BOOK OF
FAMILIAR
QUOTATIONS

over 2,500 entries

OTTENHEIMER PUBLISHERS, INC.

PREFACE

A successful writer or speaker wisely and freely falls back on the good things that have been written or said by others.

Users of these quotations are as wise as if they had originated them; for they could never originate even one-tenth of the material that they can borrow.

As you turn these pages, you will be reminded of many wise and witty sayings you have forgotten and discover others you never knew existed.

These quotations are the cream of the great writings of world literature. We hope that you enjoy this book enough to make you want to read, in their entirety, the lines from which these quotations are taken.

Ability.

Ability wins us the esteem of the true men; luck that of the people.

La Rochefoucauld.

Consider well what your strength is equal to, and what exceeds your ability.

Horace.

An able man shows his spirit by gentle words and resolute actions; he is neither hot nor timid. *Chesterfield.*

Absence.

In my Lucia's absence
Life hangs upon me, and becomes a burden;
I am ten times undone, while hope, and fear,
And grief, and rage and love rise up at once,
And with variety of pain distract me.

Addison.

O thou who dost inhabit in my breast,
Leave not the mansion. so long tenantless;
Lest growing ruinous the building fall,
And leave no memory of what it was.

Shakespeare.

Abstinence.

To set the mind above the appetites is the end of abstinence, which one of the Fathers observes to be, not a *virtue*, but the *groundwork of a virtue.* *Johnson.*

Abuse.

The bitter clamour of two eager tongues.

Shakespeare.

Account.

No reckoning made, but sent to my account
With all my imperfections on my head.

Shakespeare.

3

Acquaintance.

There is a wide difference between general acquaintance and companionship. You may salute a man and exchange compliments with him daily, yet know nothing of his character, his inmost tastes and feelings.   *Wm. Matthews.*

Acquaintances.

If a man does not make new acquaintances, as he advances through life, he will soon find himself left alone. A man should keep his friendship in constant repair.
Johnson.

Make the most of the day, by determining to spend it on *two* sorts of acquaintances only—those by whom something may be got, and those from whom something may be learned.   *Colton.*

Acquirements.

That which we acquire with the most difficulty we retain the longest; as those who have earned a fortune are usually more careful of it than those who have inherited one.   *Colton.*

Acting.

All the world's a stage.
Shakespeare.

Action.

We should often be ashamed of our very best actions, if the world only saw the motives which caused them.
La Rochefoucauld.

When we cannot act as we wish, we must act as we can.   *Terrence.*

The end of man is an action, and not a thought, though it were the noblest.
Carlyle.

Think that day lost whose low descending sun
Views from thy hand no noble action done.
Jacob Bobart.

Advise well before you begin, and when you have maturely considered, then act with promptitude.   *Sallust.*

Strong reasons make strong actions.
Shakespeare.

Actions.

Our actions are our own; their consequences belong to Heaven. *Francis.*

The evil that men do lives after them;
The good is oft interr'd with their bones.
Shakespeare.

All our actions take
Their hues from the complexion of the
heart,
As landscapes their variety from light.
W. T. Bacon.

Actions of the last age are like almanacs
of the last year. *Sir Thomas Denham.*

Act well at the moment, and you have
performed a good action to all eternity.
Lavater.

Activity.

Run, if you like, but try to keep your
breath;
Work like a man, but don't be worked to
death. *Holmes.*

Acts.

The best portion of a good man's life,
His little, nameless, unremembered acts of
kindness and of love. *Wordsworth.*

Our acts our angels are, or good or ill,
Our fatal shadows that walk by us still.
John Fletcher.

Acuteness.

The keen spirit
Seizes the prompt occasion—makes the
thought
Start into instant action, and at once
Plans and performs, resolves and executes.
Hannah Moore.

A man who knows the world will not
only make the most of everything he does
know, but of many things that he does not
know; and will gain more credit by his
adroit mode of hiding his ignorance than
the pedant by his awkward attempt to ex-
hibit his erudition. *Colton.*

5

Adversity.

Adversity borrows its sharpest sting from our impatience. *Bishop Horne.*

Adversity has the effect of eliciting talents. which in prosperous circumstances would have lain dormant. *Horace.*

The good are better made by ill,
As odors crush'd are sweeter still.
Rogers.

The firmest friendships have been formed in mutual adversity, as iron is most strongly welded by the fiercest fire.

Such a house broke!
So noble a master fallen! All gone and not
One friend to take his fortune by the arm
And go along with him. *Shakespeare.*

Adversity's sweet milk, Philosophy.
Shakespeare.

He is the most wretched of men who has never felt adversity.

Sweet are the uses of adversity,
Which like the toad, ugly and venomous,
Wears yet a precious jewel in his head;
And this our life, exempt from public haunt.
Find tongues in trees, books in the running brooks,
And good in everything. *Shakespeare.*

We ask advice, but we mean approbation. *Colton.*

Let no man presume to give advice to others that has not first given good counsel to himself. *Seneca.*

Love all, trust a few.
Do wrong to none; be able for thine enemy
Rather in power than use; and keep thy friend
Under thine own life's key; be checked for silence.
But never taxed for speech. *Shakespeare.*

The worst men often give the best advice. *Bailey.*

We give advice, but we cannot give the wisdom to profit by it. *La Rochefoucauld.*

Give thy thoughts no tongue.
Nor any unproportioned thought his act.
Be thou familiar, but by no means vulgar.
The friends thou hast, and their adoption
    tried,
Grapple them to thy soul with hooks of
    steel;
But do not dull thy palm with entertain-
    ment
Of each new-hatched, unfledged comrade.
    Beware
Of entrance to a quarrel; but, being in,
Bear it that the opposer may beware of
    thee.
Give every man thine ear, but few thy
    voice.
Take each man's censure, but reserve thy
    judgment.
Costly thy habit as thy purse can buy,
But not expressed in fancy; rich, not
    gaudy;
For the apparel oft proclaims the man.
Neither a borrower nor a lender be,
For loan oft loses both itself and friend;
And borrowing dulls the edge of hus-
    bandry.
This above all: To thine own self be true;
And it must follow, as the night the day,
Thou cans't not then be false to any man.

Shakespeare.

He who can take advice is sometimes
superior to him who can give it.

Von Knebel.

Let no man value at a little price
A virtuous woman's counsel; her winged
    spirit
Is feathered often times with heavenly
    words,
And, like her beauty, ravishing and pure.

Chapman.

Affection.

Fathers alone a father's heart can know
What secret tides of still enjoyment flow
When brothers love, but if their hate suc-
    ceeds,
They wage the war, but 'tis the father
    bleeds.   *Young.*

Affections.

Of all the tyrants the world affords,
Our own affections are the fiercest lords.
Earl of Sterling.

O you much partial gods!
Why gave ye men affections, and not power
To govern them? *Ludovick Barry.*

Nothing can occur beyond the strength
of faith to sustain, or, transcending the resources of religion, to relieve. *Binney.*

Man is born to trouble, as the sparks fly
upward. *Job* v. 7.

Age.

Age sits with decent grace upon his visage,
And worthily becomes his silver locks;
He bears the marks of many years well
    spent,
Of virtue truth well tried, and wise exper-
    ience. *Rowe.*

As you are old and reverend, you should
be wise. *Shakespeare.*

These are the effects of doting age,
Vain doubts, and idle cares, and over caution. *Dryden.*

But an old age serene and bright,
And lovely as a Lapland night,
Shall lead thee to thy grave.
            Wordsworth.

How blest is he who crowns, in shades like
    these,
A youth of labor with an age of ease.
            Goldsmith.

Eternal sunshine settles on its head.
            Goldsmith.

Care keeps his watch in every old man's
    eye. *Shakespeare.*

When men grow virtuous in their old
age, they are merely making a sacrifice to
God of the Devil's leavings. *Swift.*

            Last scene of all
That ends this strange, eventful history,
Is second childishness, and mere oblivion;
Sans teeth, sans eyes, sans taste, sans
    everything. *Shakespeare.*

These old fellows have
Their ingratitude in them hereditary;
Their blood is caked, 'tis cold, it seldom
 flows;
'Tis lack of kindly warmth, they are not
 kind,
And nature, as it grows toward earth,
Is fashion'd for the journey—dull and
 heavy.   *Shakespeare.*

Every man desires to live long; but no
man would be old.   *Swift.*

Age is a tyrant, who forbids, at the pen-
alty of life, all the pleasures of youth.
  La Rochefoucauld.

Ambition.

Ambition is an idol, on whose wings
Great minds are carried only to extreme;
To be sublimely great or to be nothing.
  Southey.

O cursed ambition, thou devouring bird,
How dost thou from the field of honesty
Pick every grain of profit or delight,
And mock the reaper's toil!   *Havard.*

What is ambition? 'Tis a glorious cheat.
Angels of light walk not so dazzlingly
The sapphire walls of heaven.   *Willis.*

Dream after dream ensues,
And still they dream that they shall still
 succeed,
And still are disappointed.   *Cowper.*

Ambition's like a circle on the water,
Which never ceases to enlarge itself,
'Till by broad spreading it disperse to
 nought.   *Shakespeare.*

Accurst ambition,
How dearly I have bought you.
  Dryden.

Airy ambition, soaring high.   *Sheffield.*

Why dost thou court that baneful pest, ambition?   *Potter.*

—— brave thirst of fame his bosom warms.
  Churchill.

Ah! curst ambition! to thy lures we owe,
All the great ills that mortals bear below.
  Teckell.

The dropsy'd thirst of empire, wealth or
    fame.   *Nugent.*

The glorious frailty of the noble mind.
                            Hoole.

No bounds his headlong, vast ambition
    knows.   *Rowe.*

Ambition is like love, impatient
Both of delays and rivals.
                            Denham.

———————— ambition, idly vain ;
Revenge and malice swell her train.
                            Penrose.

Vaulting ambition which o'erleaps itself.
                            Shakespeare.

What's all the gaudy glitter of a crown ?
What but the glaring meteor of ambition,
That leads the wretch benighted in his
    errors,
Points to the gulf and shines upon destruc-
    tion ?   *Brooke.*

Who soars too near the sun, with golden
    wings,
Melts them ; to ruin his own fortune brings.
                            Shakespeare.

Farewell, a long farewell, to all my great-
    ness !

This is the state of man. To-day he puts
    forth

The tender leaves of hope ; to-morrow blos-
    soms,

And bears his blushing honors thick upon
    him ;

The third day comes a frost, a killing
    frost.   *Shakespeare.*

                    'Tis a common proof,
That lowliness is young ambition's ladder,
Wherto the climber upwards turns his
    face ;
But when he once attains the utmost
    round,
He then unto the ladder turns his back,
Looks in the clouds, scorning the base de-
    grees
By which he did ascend.   *Shakespeare.*

Ambition is a lust that's never quenched,
Grows more inflamed, and madder by en-
            joyment.   *Otway.*

A slave has but one master; the ambitious man has as many masters as there are persons whose aid may contribute to the advancement of his fortune.

La Bruyère.

Our natures are like oil; compound us with anything,
Yet will we strive to swim at the top.

Beaumont and Fletcher.

Dreams, indeed, are ambition; for the very substance of the ambitious is merely the shadow of a dream. And I hold ambition of so airy and light a quality, that it is but a shadow's shadow. *Shakespeare.*

Oh, sons of earth! attempt ye still to rise.
By mountains pil'd on mountains to the skies?
Heaven still with laughter the vain toil surveys,
And buries madmen in the heaps they raise. *Pope.*

Amusements.

The mind ought sometimes to be amused, that it may the better return to thought, and to itself. *Phaedrus.*

Ancestry.

I am one
Who finds within me a nobility
That spurns the idle pratings of the great,
And their mean boast of what their fathers were,
While they themselves are fools effeminate,
The scorn of all who know the worth of mind
And virtue. *Percival.*

The man who has not anything to boast of but his illustrious ancestors, is like a potato—the only thing belonging to him is under ground. *Sir T. Overbury.*

Angels.

So dear to heaven is saintly chastity,
That when a soul is found sincerely so
A thousand liveried angels lackey her.

Milton.

11

Man hath two attendant angels
    Ever waiting by his side,
With him wheresoe'r he wanders,
    Wheresoe'r his feet abide;
One to warn him when he darkleth,
    And rebuke him if he stray;
One to leave him to his nature,
    And so let him go his way.   *Prince.*

A guardian angel o'er his life presides,
Doubling his pleasures and his cares divid-
            ing.   *Rogers.*

We are ne'er like angels 'till our passion
    dies.   *Dekker.*

Fools rush in where angels fear to tread.
                        Pope.

Anger.

Be ye angry and sin not; let not the sun
go down upon your wrath.   *Eph.* iv, 26.

            Anger
Is blood, pour'd and perplexed into a froth.
                    Davenant.

My rage is not malicious; like a spark
Of fire by steel inforced out of a flint
It is no sooner kindled, but extinct.
                        Goffe.

        There is not in nature
A thing that makes a man so deform'd, so
    beastly,
As doth intemperate anger.
                Webster's Duchess of Malfi.

To be angry, is to revenge the fault of
others upon ourselves.   *Pope.*

The intoxication of anger, like that of
the grape, shows us to others, but hides us
from ourselves, and we injure our own
cause, in the opinion of the world, when we
too passionately and eagerly defend it.
                        Colton.

When a man is wrong and won't admit
it, he always gets angry.   *Haliburton.*

My indignation, like th' imprisoned fire,
Pent in the troubled breast of glowing
    Ætna,
Burnt deep and silent.   *Thomson.*

If anger is not restrained, it is frequently more hurtful to us, than the injury that
provokes it. *Seneca.*
O that my tongue were in the thunder's
mouth !
Then with a passion would I shake the
world. *Shakespeare.*

Angling.

In genial spring, beneath the quiv'ring
shade,
Where cooling vapors breathe along the
mead,
The patient fisher takes his silent stand,
Intent, his angle trembling in his hand ;
With looks unmoved, he hopes the scaly
breed,
And eyes the dancing cork and bending
reed. *Pope.*

I in these flowery meads would be ;
These crystal streams would solace me ;
To whose harmonious, bubbling noise
I with my angle would rejoice.
Isaac Walton.

Animals.

Let cavillers deny
That brutes have reason ; sure 'tis some-
thing more,
'Tis heaven directs, and stratagems in-
spires
Beyond the short extent of human thought.
Somerville.

Answering.

Any man that can write, may answer a
letter. *Shakespeare.*

Anticipation.

By the pricking of my thumbs
Something wicked this way comes.
Shakespeare.

Antipathy.

Some men there are love not a gaping pig ;
Some that are mad, if they behold a cat.
Masterless passion sways it to the mood,
Of what it likes or loathes *Shakespeare.*

13

Antiquary.

They say he sits
All day in contemplation of a statue.
With ne'er a nose, and dotes on the decays
With greater love than the self-lov'd Nar-
cissus
Did on his beauty.   *Shakerly Marmyon.*

Antiquity.

Time's gradual touch
Has moulder'd into beauty many a tower
Which when it frown'd with all its battle-
ments.
Was only terrible.   *Mason.*

All those things which are now held to
be of the greatest antiquity, were at one
time new; and what we to-day hold up by
example, will rank hereafter as a precedent.   *Tacitus.*

Anxiety.

It is not work that kills men; it is
worry. Work is healthy; you can hardly
put more upon a man than he can bear.
Worry is rust upon the blade. It is not
the revolution that destroys the machinery,
but the friction. Fear secretes acids; but
love and trust are sweet juices.
      Beecher.

Apology.

What! shall this speech be spoke for our
      excuse?
Or shall we on without apology?
      Shakespeare.

Appeal.

And here I stand; judge, my masters.
      Shakespeare.

Appearance.

He has, I know not what
Of greatness in his looks, and of high fate
That almost awes me.   *Dryden.*

Within the oyster's shell uncouth
The purest pearl may hide,
Trust me you'll find a heart of truth
Within that rough inside.
      Mrs. Osgood.

'Tis not the fairest form that holds
  The mildest, purest soul within ;
'Tis not the richest plant that holds
  The sweetest fragrance in.   *Dawes.*

Appearances.

     Appearances deceive
And this one maxim is a standing rule :
Men are not what they seem.   *Havard.*

  The ass is still an ass, e'en though he
wears a lion's hide.

  The chameleon may change its color, but
it is the chameleon still.

The world is still deceived by ornament.
In law, what plea so tainted and corrupt,
But being seasoned with a gracious voice,
Obscures the show of error ?   In religion,
What damn'd error, but some sober brow
Will bless it and approve it with a text,
Hiding the grossness with fair ornament?
There is no vice so simple, but assumes
Some mark of virtue on its outward parts.
How many cowards, whose hearts are all
    as false
As stairs of sand, wear yet upon their
    chins
The beards of Hercules, and frowning
    Mars ;
Who inward search'd have livers white as
    milk?
And these assume but valor's excrement,
To render them redoubted. Look on beauty,
And you shall see 'tis purchas'd by the
    weight ;
Which therein works a miracle in nature,
Making them lightest that wear most of it.
So are those crisped, snaky, golden locks,
Which make such wanton gambols with the
    wind,
Upon supposed fairness, often known
To be the dowry of a second head,
The skull that bred them, in the sepulchre.
Thus ornament is but the guilded shore
To the most dangerous sea ; the beauteous
    scarf
Veiling an Indian beauty ; in a word,
The seeming truth which cunning times
    put on
To entrap the wisest.   *Shakespeare.*

15

Appetite.

Now good digestion wait on appetite,
And health on both.   *Shakespeare*

Applause.

Applause is the spur of noble minds, the
end and aim of weak ones.   *Colton.*

Apple.

He kept him as the apple of his eye.
                    Deut. xxxii, 10.

Appreciation.

A primrose on the river's brim,
  Or by the cottage door,
A yellow primrose was to him,
  And it was nothing more.
                    Wordsworth.

Apprehensions.

Better to be despised for too anxious ap-
prehensions, than ruined by too confident a
security.   *Burke.*

Appropriation.

It is a special trick of low cunning to
squeeze out knowledge from a modest man,
who is eminent in any science, and then to
use it as legally acquired, and pass the
source in total silence.   *Horace Walpole.*

Aptitude.

I cannot draw a cart, nor eat dried oats;
If it be man's work I will do it.
                    Shakespeare.

Architect.

Every man is the architect of his own
fortune.   *Appius Claudius.*

Architecture.

Architecture is the printing press of all
ages, and gives a history of the state of
the society in which it was erected.
                    Lady Morgan.

Argument.

Who shall decide when doctors disagree,
And sound casuists doubt like you and me?
                    Pope.
The Devil can quote scripture for his pur-
pose.   *Shakespeare.*

Be calm in arguing; for fierceness makes
Error a fault, and truth discourtesy.
Why should I feel another man's mistakes
More than his sickness or poverty?
In love I should; but anger is not love,
Nor wisdom neither; therefore gently
    move.
Calmness is great advantage; he that lets
Another chafe may warm him at his fire,
Mark all his wand'rings and enjoy his
    frets,
As cunning fencers suffer heat to tire.
                  Herbert.

    A man convinced against his will
    Is of the same opinion still.   *Butler.*
No argument can be drawn from the
abuse of a thing against its use.   *Latin.*
In arguing, too, the parson owned his skill,
For even tho' vanquish'd he could argue
    still.   *Goldsmith.*

He'd undertake to prove, by force
    O' argument, a man's no horse.
He'd prove a buzzard is no fowl,
And that a lord may be an owl,
A calf an alderman, a goose a justice,
And rooks committeemen and trustees.
                  Butler.

Arguments.

Examples I could cite you more;
But be contented with these four;
For when one's proofs are aptly chosen
Four are as valid as four dozen.   *Prior.*

Army.

All in a moment through the gloom were
    seen
Ten thousand banners rise into the air,
With orient colors waving: With them
    rose
A forest huge of spears, and thronging
    helms
Appear'd, and serried shields and thick
    array
Of depth immeasurable.   *Milton.*

Artifice.

It is sometimes necessary to play the
fool to avoid being deceived by cunning
men.   *La Rochefoucauld.*

Artist.

A flattering painter, who made it his care
To draw men as they ought to be, not as
they are. *Goldsmith.*

Ascendency.

Whatever natural right men have to
freedom and independency, it is manifest
that some men have a natural ascendency
over others. *Greville.*

Aspect.

The tartness of his face sours ripe grapes.
Shakespeare.

Assertions.

There is nothing as cheap and weak in
debate as assertion that is not backed by
fact.

Assignation.

An assignation sweetly made,
With gentle whispers in the dark.
Francis.

Associates.

Choose the company of your superiors,
whenever you can have it; that is the right
and true pride. *Lord Chesterfield.*

He who comes from the kitchen, smells
of its smoke; and he who adheres to a
sect, has something of its cant; the college air pursues the student; and dry in-
humanity him who herds with literary
pedants. *Lavater.*

Associations.

There's not a wind but whispers of thy
name;
And not a flow'r that grows beneath the
moon,
But in its hues and fragrance tells a tale
Of thee, my love. *Barry Cornwall.*

Astonishment.

I could a tale unfold, whose lightest word
Would harrow up thy soul; freeze thy
young blood;
Make thy two eyes, like stars, start from
their spheres;
Thy knotted and combined locks to part,
And each particular hair to stand on end,
Like quills upon the fretful porcupine.
Shakespeare.

Astronomy.

The contemplation of celestial things will make a man both speak and think more sublimely and magnificently when he descends to human affairs. *Cicero.*

Atheism.

Atheism is the result of ignorance and pride; of strong sense and feeble reasons; of good eating and ill-living. It is the plague of society, the corrupter of manners, and the underminer of property.
Jeremy Collier.

There is no being eloquent for atheism. In that exhausted receiver the mind cannot use its wings —the clearest proof that it is out of its element. *Hare.*

Atheism is rather in the life than in the heart of man. *Bacon.*

Atheist.

No atheist, as such, can be a true friend, an affectionate relation, or a loyal subject. *Dr. Bentley.*

By night an atheist half believes a God.
Young.

Atmosphere.

When you find that flowers and shrubs will not endure a certain atmosphere, it is a very significant hint to the human creature to remove out of that neighborhood.
Mayhew.

Attention.

Lend thy serious hearing to what I shall unfold. *Shakespeare.*

Author.

Never write on a subject without having first read yourself full on it; and never read on a subject 'till you have thought yourself hungry on it. *Richter.*

If an author write better than his contemporaries, they will term him a plagiarist; if as well, a pretender; but if worse, he may stand some chance of commendation as a genius of some promise, from whom much may be expected by a due attention to their good counsel and advice.
Colton.

Authority.

Man, proud man!
Drest in a little brief authority,
Most ignorant of what he's most assur'd,
His glassy essence, like an angry ape,
Plays such fantastic tricks before high
    heaven
As make the angels weep.   *Shakespeare.*

Authority intoxicates,
And makes mere sots of magistrates.
The fumes of it invade the brain,
And make men giddy, proud and vain;
By this the fool commands the wise
The noble with the base complies.
The sot assumes the rule of wit,
And cowards make the base submit.
                    Butler.

Authorship.

The two most engaging powers of an author are to make *new* things *familiar,* and *familiar* things *new.*   *Johnson.*

None but an author knows an author's
    cares,
Or fancy's fondness for the child she bears.
                  Cowper.

'Tis pleasant, sure, to see one's name in
    print;
A book's a book, although there's nothing
    in't.   *Byron.*

Autumn.

Then came the autumne, all in yellow clad,
As though he joy'd in his plenteous store,
Laden with fruits that made him laugh, full
    glad
That he had banished hunger, which tofore
Had by the belly oft him pinched sore;
Upon his head a wreath that was enrol'd
With ears of corne of every sort, he bore,
And in his hand a sickle did he holde,
To reape the ripened fruit the which the
    earth had yold.   *Spenser.*

Thrice happy time,
Best portion of the various year, in which
Nature rejoiceth, smiling on her works
Lovely, to full perfection wrought.
                Phillips.

Avarice.

It may be remarked for the comfort of honest poverty, that avarice reigns most in those who have but few good qualities to recommend them. This is a weed that will grow in a barren soil. *Hughes.*

Because men believe not in Providence, therefore they do so greedily scrape and hoard. They do not believe in any reward for charity, therefore they will part with nothing. *Barrow.*

O, cursed love of gold; when for thy sake,
The fool throws up his interest in both
   worlds,
First starved in this, then damn'd in that
   to come. *Blair.*

Extreme avarice is nearly always mistaken; there is no passion which is oftener further away from its mark, nor upon which the present has so much power to the prejudice of the future. *La Rochefoucauld.*

Avarice is always poor, but poor by her own fault. *Johnson.*

'Tis strange the miser should his cares employ
To gain those riches he can ne'er enjoy.
Pope.

Aversion.

I do not love thee, Doctor Fell.
The reason why, I cannot tell;
But this alone I know full well
I do not love thee, Doctor Fell.
Tom Brown.

Awkwardness.

Not all the pumice of the polish'd town
Can smooth the roughness of the barnyard
   clown;
Rich, honor'd, titled, he betrays his race
By this one mark—he's awkward in his
   face. *Holmes.*

Axe.

When I see a merchant over-polite to his customer, begging them to take a little brandy, and throwing his goods on the counter, thinks I, that man has an axe to grind. *Franklin (Poor Richard.)*

Babbler.

Fie! what a spendthrift he is of his
tongue! *Shakespeare.*

Badness.

Damnable, both sides rogue.
Shakespeare.

Bag.

It is hard for an empty bag to stand upright. *Franklin (Poor Richard.)*

Ball.

A thousand hearts beat happily; and when
Music arose with its voluptuous swell
Soft eyes looked love to eyes that spake
again,
And all went merry as a marriage bell.
Byron.

I saw her at a country ball,
There, when the sound of flute and fiddle,
Gave signal sweet in that old hall,
Of hands across and down the middle.
Her's was the subtlest spell by far
Of all that sets young hearts romancing;
She was our queen, our rose, our star;
And when she danced—oh, heaven, her
dancing! *Praed.*

Ballads.

I knew a very wise man that believed
that, if a man were permitted to make all
the ballads, he need not care who should
make the laws of a nation.
Fletcher of Saltoun.

Ballot.

As lightly falls
As snow flakes fall upon the sod,
But executes a freeman's will,
As lightning does the will of God.
Halleck.

Banishment.

All places that the eye of heaven visits,
Are, to a wise man, ports and happy

havens.
Teach thy necessity to reason thus:
There is no virtue like necessity.

Shakespeare.

Banquet.

A table richly spread in regal mode,
With dishes piled, and meats of noblest
    sort,
And savor; beasts of chase, or fowl of
    game,
In pastry built, or from the spit, or boil'd
Gris-amber-steam'd; all fish from sea or
    shore,
Freshet or purling brook, for which was
    drain'd
Pontus, and Lucrine bay, and Afric coast

Milton.

Bashfulness.

So sweet the blush of bashfulness
Even pity scarce can wish it less.

Byron

There are two distinct sorts of what we
call bashfulness; *this,* the awkwardness of
a booby, which a few steps into the world
will convert into the pertness of a cox
comb; *that,* a consciousness. which the
most delicate feelings produce, and the
most extensive knowledge cannot always
remove. *Mackenzie.*

Battle.

His back against a rock he bore.
And firmly placed his foot before;
"Come one, come all! this rock shall fly
From its firm base as soon as I." *Scott.*
Now night her course began, and over
    heaven
Inducing darkness, grateful truce, impos'd
Her silence on the odious din of war;
Under her cloudy covert hath retired
Victor and vanquish'd. *Milton.*
Hark! the death-denouncing trumpet
    sounds
The fatal charge, and shouts proclaim the
    onset;

Destruction rushes dreadful to the field,
And bathes itself in blood; havoc let loose
Now undistinguish'd rages all around,
While ruin, seated on her dreary throne,
Sees the plain strewed with subjects truly
    hers,
Breathless and cold.   *Harvard.*

That awful pause, dividing life from death,
Struck for an instant on the hearts of men,
Thousands of whom were drawing their
    last breath !
A moment all will be life again.
* * * * * * one moment more,
The death-cry drowning in the battle's
    roar.   *Byron.*

         This day hath made
Much work for tears in many an English
    mother,
Whose sons lie scatter'd on the bleeding
    ground;
Many a widow's husband groveling lies,
Coldly embracing the discolor'd earth.
            Shakespeare.

When Greeks join'd Greeks, then was the
    tug of war;
The labour'd battle sweat, and conquest
    bled.   *Lee.*

Beard.

It has no bush below;
Marry a little wool, as much as an unripe
Peach doth wear;
Just enough to speak him drawing towards
    a man.   *Suckling.*
He that hath a beard is more than a youth;
And he that hath none is less than a man.
            Shakespeare.

Beautiful.

The beautiful are never desolate,
But some one always loves them.
            Bailey.

Beauty.

        O she is all perfection,
All that the blooming earth can send forth
    fair,
All that the gaudy heavens could drop
    down glorious.   *Lee.*

When I approach
Her loveliness, so absolute she seems,
And in herself complete, so well to know
Her own, that what she wills to do or say,
Seems wisest, virtuousest, discretest, best;
All higher knowledge in her presence falls
Degraded. Wisdom in discourse with her
Loses, discount'nanc'd, and like folly
  shows.   *Milton.*

Nature was here so lavish of her store,
That she bestow'd until she had no more.
                                        Brown.

Oh! she has a beauty might ensnare
A conqueror's soul, and make him leave his
  crown
At random, to be scuffled for by slaves.
                                        Otway.

Grace was in all her steps, heav'n in her
  eye,
In every gesture dignity and love. *Milton.*

Beauty is a witch,
Against whose charms faith melteth into
  blood.   *Shakespeare.*

Her eyes, her lips, her cheeks, her shapes,
  her features,
Seem to be drawn by love's own hand; by
  love
Himself in love.   *Dryden.*

  The criterion of true beauty is, that it
increases on examination; of false, that it
lessens. There is something, therefore, in
true beauty that corresponds with the right
reason, and it is not merely the creature
of fancy.   *Greville.*

Beauty, like ice, our footing does betray;
Who can tread sure on the smooth, slip-
  pery way?
Pleased with the surface, we glide swiftly
  on,
And see the dangers that we cannot shun.
                                        Dryden.

I long not for the cherries on the tree,
So much as those which on a lip I see;
And more affection bear I to the rose
That in a cheek than in a garden grows.
                                        Randolph.

A thing of beauty is a joy forever,
Its loveliness increases; it will never
Pass into nothingness.   *Keats.*

O fatal beauty! why art thou bestow'd
On hapless woman still to make her
      wretched!
Betray'd by thee, how many are undone!
                              Patterson.

For her own person,
It beggar'd all description; she did lie
In her pavilion,
O'er-picturing that Venus, where we see
The fancy outwork nature. *Shakespeare.*

That is the best part of beauty which a
picture cannot express.   *Bacon.*

Beauty is worse than wine; it intoxicates both the holder and the beholder.
                              Zimmerman.

Beauty is truth, truth beauty—that is all
Ye know on earth, and all ye need to know.
                              Keats.

When I forget that the stars shine in air,
When I forget that beauty is in stars—
Shall I forget thy beauty.   *Thomson.*

But then her face
So lovely, yet so arch, so full of mirth,
The overflowings of an innocent heart.
                              Rogers.

All orators are dumb when beauty plead-
eth.   **Shakespeare.**

Socrates called beauty, a short lived
tyranny; Plato, a privilege of nature;
Theophrastes, a silent cheat; Theocritus,
a delightful prejudice; Carneades, a solitary kingdom; Domitian said that nothing
was more grateful; Aristotle affirmed that
beauty was better than all the letters of
recommendation in the world; Homer, that
'twas a glorious gift of nature; and Ovid
alluding to him, calls it a favor bestowed
by the Gods.

Remember if you marry for beauty, thou
bindest thyself all thy life for that which,
perchance, will neither last nor please thee
one year: and when thou hast it, it will
be to thee of no price at all.   *Raleigh.*

Without the smile from partial beauty won,
O, what were man! a world without a sun!
                    Campbell.

              Beauty,
That transitory flower; even while it lasts
Palls on the roving sense, when held too
    near,
Or dwelling there too long; by fits it
    pleases,
And smells at distance best; its sweets
    familiar
By frequent converse, soon grow dull and
    cloy you.   *Jeffry.*

    The mate for beauty should be a man
and not a money chest.   *Bulwer.*

Ye tradeful merchants! that with weary
    toil,
Do seek most precious things to make you
    gaine,
And both the Indies of their treasures
    spoil :
What needeth you to seek so far in vain?
For lo! my love doth in herself contain
All this world's riches that may far be
    found ;
If saphyrs, lo! her eyes be saphyrs plain ;
If rubies, lo! her lips be rubies sound ;
If pearls, her teeth be pearls, both pure
    and round ;
If ivory, her forehead's ivory I ween ;
If gold, her locks are finest gold on
    ground ;
If silver, her fair hands are silver sheen :
But that which fairest is, but few behold,
Her mind, adorn'd with virtues manifold.
                    Spenser.

    Every trait of beauty may be traced to
some virtue, as to innocence, candour, gen-
erosity, modesty, and heroism. *St. Pierre.*

Beauty is but a vain and doubtful good,
A shining gloss, that fadeth suddenly,
A flower that dies when first it 'gins to bud,
A brittle glass, that's broken presently :
A doubtful good, a gloss a glass, a flower,
Lost, faded, broken, dead within an hour.
                    Shakespeare.

Beauty is as summer fruits, which are easy to corrupt and cannot last; and for the most part it makes a dissolute youth, and an age a little out of countenance; but if it light well, it makes virtue shine and vice blush. *Bacon.*

Honesty coupled to beauty, is to have honey sauce to sugar. *Shakespeare.*

What is beauty? Not the show
Of shapely limbs and features. No;
These are but flowers
That have their dated hours,
To breathe their momentary sweets and go.
'Tis the stainless soul within
That outshines the fairest skin.
Sir A. Hunt.

Beauty. without virtue, is like a flower without perfume. *From the French.*

Bed.

Bed is a bundle of paradoxes; we go to it with reluctance, yet we quit it with regret; and we make up our minds every night to leave it early, but we make up our bodies every morning to keep it late.
Colton.

Bed-Chamber.

Sweet pillows, sweetest bed;
A chamber deaf to noise, and blind to light;
A rosy garland, and a weary head.
Sir Philip Sydney.

Bee.

How doth the little busy bee
  Improve each shining hour,
And gather honey all the day
  From every opening flower. *Watts.*

Many colored, sunshine loving, spring-betokening bee!
Yellow bee, so mad for love of early blooming flowers!
Till thy waxen cells be full, fair fall thy work and thee,
Buzzing round the sweetly-smelling garden plots and flowers.
Professor Wilson.

Bees.

Even bees, the little alms-men of spring
    bowers,
Know there is richest juice in poison-
    flowers.   *Keats.*

         So work the honey-bees;
Creatures, that by a rule in nature teach
The art of order to a peopled kingdom.
They have a king and officers of sorts;
Where some, like magistrates, correct at
    home;
Others, like merchants, venture trade
    abroad;
Others, like soldiers, armed in their stings,
Make boot upon the summer's velvet buds;
Which pillage they, with merry march,
    bring home,
To the tent royal of their emperor;
Who, busied in his majesty, surveys
The singing masons building roofs of gold;
The civil citizens kneading up the honey;
The poor mechanic porters crowding in
Their heavy burdens at his narrow gate;
The sad-ey'd justice, with his surly hum,
Delivering o'er to executors pale
The lazy yawning drone.   *Shakespeare.*

Beggar.

The beggar, as he stretch'd his shrivel'd
    hand,
Rais'd not his eyes and those who dropp'd
    the mite
Pass'd on unnoticed.   *Bailey.*

The adage must be verified—
That beggars mounted, run their horse to
    death.   *Shakespeare.*

Well, while I am a beggar, I will rail,
And say,—there is no sin, but to be rich;
And being rich my virtue then shall be,
To say,—there is no vice but beggary.
                   Shakespeare.

Behavior.

   Levity of behavior is the bane of all that
is good and virtuous.   *Seneca.*

   What is becoming is honorable, and
what is honorable is becoming.   *Tully.*

29

Never put off till to-morrow what you can do to-day.

Never trouble another for what you can do yourself.

Never spend your money before you have it.

Never buy what you do not want because it is cheap.

Pride costs us more than hunger, thirst, and cold.

We seldom repent having eaten too little.

Nothing is troublesome that we do willingly.

How much pain the evils have cost us that have never happened!

Take things always by the smooth handle.

When angry, count ten before you speak: if very angry, a hundred.   *Jefferson.*

Belief.

'Tis with our judgments as our watches;
  none
Are just alike, yet each believes his own.
                    Pope.

You believe that easily which you hope for earnestly.   *Terence.*

Bells.

How soft the music of those village bells,
Falling at intervals upon the ear
In cadence sweet! now dying all away,
Now pealing loud again and louder still,
Clear and sonorous as the gale comes on,
With easy force it opens all the cells
Where memory slept.   *Cowper.*

Benefactor.

And he gave it for his opinion, that whoever could make two ears of corn, or two blades of grass to grow upon a spot of ground, where only one grew before, would deserve better of mankind, and do more essential service to his country, than the whole race of politicians put together.
                    Swift.

Beneficence.

Men resemble the gods in nothing so much as in doing good to their fellow creatures.   *Cicero.*

Benevolence.

The conqueror is regarded with awe, the wise man commands our esteem, but it is the benevolent man who wins our affection.
From the French.

A poor man served by thee, shall make thee rich.   *Mrs. Browning.*

Think not the good,
The gentle deeds of mercy thou hast done,
Shall die forgotten all; the poor, the pris-
   'ner,
The fatherless, the friendless, and the
   widow,
Who daily own the bounty of thy hand,
Shall cry to heav'n and pull a blessing on
   thee.   *Rowe.*

The truly generous is the truly wise;
And he who loves not others lives unblest.
Home.

Bible.

This Book, this Holy Book, on every line,
Mark'd with the seal of high divinity,
On every leaf bedew'd with drops of love
Divine, and with the eternal heraldry
And signature of God Almighty stamp'd
From first to last; this ray of sacred light,
This lamp, from off the everlasting throne,
Mercy took down, and in the night of time
Stood, casting on the dark her gracious
   bow;
And evermore beseeching men with tears
And earnest sighs, to read, believe and live.
Pollok.

It has God for its author, salvation for its end, and truth, without any mixture of error, for its matter;—it is all pure, all sincere; nothing too much, nothing wanting.   *Locke.*

The Scriptures teach us the best way of living, the noblest way of suffering, and the most comfortable way of dying.
Flavel.

A glory gilds the sacred page,
　Majestic like the sun,
It gives a light to every age;
　It gives, but borrows none.
Cowper.

Within that awful volume lies
The mystery of mysteries. 　*Scott.*

Bigotry.

She has no head, and cannot think; no
heart, and cannot feel. When she moves,
it is in wrath; when she pauses, it is amid
ruin; her prayers are curses—her God is a
demon—her communion is death—her ven-
geance is eternity—her decalogue written
in the blood of her victims; and if she
stops for a moment in her infernal flight,
it is upon a kindred rock, to whet her
vulture fang for a more sanguinary desolation. 　*Daniel O'Connell.*

To follow foolish precedents, and wink
With both our eyes is easier than to think.
Cowper.

Bird.

A light broke in upon my soul—
　It was the carol of a bird;
It ceased—and then it came again
　The sweetest song ear ever heard.
Byron.

Birth.

When real nobleness accompanies that
imaginary one of birth, the imaginary
seems to mix with real, and becomes real
too. 　*Greville.*

Birthday.

Yet all I've learnt from hours rife,
　With painful brooding here,
Is, that amid this mortal strife,
　The lapse of every year
But takes away a hope from life,
　And adds to death a fear.
Hoffman.

Blessings.

The dews of heaven fall thick in blessings on her. 　*Shakespeare.*
How blessings brighten as they take
their flight! 　*Young.*

Blindness.

He whom nature thus bereaves,
　Is ever fancy's favorite child;
For thee enchanted dreams she weaves
　Of changeful beauty, bright and wild.
Mrs. Osgood.

Blockhead.

A bee is not a busier animal than a
blockhead. *Pope.*

Bluntness.

　　This is some fellow,
Who having been prais'd for bluntness,
　doth affect
A saucy roughness, and constrains the
　garb,
Quite from his nature: he can't flatter, he!
An honest mind and plain,—he must speak
　truth!
And they will take it so; if not he's plain.
These kind of knaves I know, which in
　this plainness
Harbor more craft, and far corrupter ends,
Than twenty silly, duckling observants,
That stretch their duty nicely.
Shakespeare.

I have neither wit, nor words, nor worth,
Nor actions, nor utterance, nor the power
　of speech,
To stir men's blood: I only speak right on.
Shakespeare.

Blushes.

The heart's meteors tilting in the face.
Shakespeare.

　Give me the eloquent cheek,
　　When blushes burn and die
　Like thine its changes speak,
　　The spirit's purity. *Mrs. Osgood.*
————the blush is formed—and flies—
Nor owns reflection's calm control;
It comes, it deepens—fades and dies,
　A gush of feeling from the soul.
Mrs. Dinnies.

The blush is Nature's alarm at the approach of sin and her testimony to the
dignity of virtue. *Fuller.*

Confusion thrill'd me then, and secret joy
Fast throbbing, stole its treasure from
    my heart,
And mantling upward, turn'd my face to
    crimson.   *Brooke.*

Boasting.

When you begin with so much pomp and
    show,
Why is the end so little and so low?
                Roscommon.

The empty vessel makes the greatest
sound.   *Shakespeare.*

For men (it is reported) dash and vapor
Less on the field of battle than on paper.
Thus in the hist'ry of dire campaign
More carnage loads the newspaper than
    plain.   *Dr. Wolcott.*

Body.

What! know ye not that your body is
the temple of the Holy Ghost which is in
you, which ye have of God: and ye are not
your own?   *Cor.* vi, 19.

For of the soul the body form doth take,
For soul is form, and doth the body make.
                Spenser.

Books.

Books are a guide in youth, and an en-
tertainment for age. They support us
under solitude, and keep us from becoming
a burden to ourselves. They help us to
forget the crossness of men and things,
compose our cares and our passions, and
lay our disappointments asleep. When we
are weary of the living, we may repair to
the dead, who have nothing of peevish-
ness, pride or design in their conversation.
                Collier.

Books should to one of these four ends
    conduce,
For wisdom, piety, delight or use.
                Denham.

—————— The place that does
Contain my books, the best companions, is
To me a glorious court, where hourly I
Converse with the old sages and philoso-
    phers;

And sometimes for variety, I confer
With kings and emperors, and weigh their
  counsels;
Calling their victories, if unjustly got,
Unto a strict account: and in my fancy,
Deface their ill-plac'd statutes. *Fletcher.*

Books are men of higher stature,
And the only men that speak aloud for
  future times to hear! *Mrs. Browning.*

Books, as Dryden aptly termed them, are
spectacles to read nature. * * They
teach us to understand and feel what we
see, to decipher and syllable the hiero-
glyphics of the sense. *Hare.*

Books cannot always please, however good,
Minds are not ever craving for their food.
Crabbe.

He that will have no books but those
that are scarce, evinces about as correct a
taste in literature as he would do in friendship, who would have no friends but those
whom all the rest of the world have sent
to Coventry. *Colton.*

As good almost kill a man, as kill a good
book; who kills a man, kills a reasonable
creature, God's image; but he who destroys a good book, kills reason itself.
Milton.

Reading maketh a full man, conference
a ready man, and writing an exact man.
Bacon.

History makes men wise; poets, witty;
the mathematics, subtile; natural philosophy, deep; moral, grave; logic and rhetoric
able to contend. *Bacon.*

A good book is the precious life-blood of
a master spirit, embalmed and treasured
up on purpose to a life beyond life.
Milton.

'Tis in books the chief
Of all perfections to be plain and brief.
Butler.

Some books are to be tasted, others to
be swallowed, and some few to be chewed
and digested. *Bacon.*

35

Many books require no thought from those who read them, for a very simple reason;—they made no such demand upon those who wrote them. Those works, therefore, are the most valuable that set our thinking faculties in the fullest operation. *Colton.*

I have somewhere seen it observed, that we should make the same use of a book that the bee does of a flower: she steals sweets from it, but does not injure it.
Colton.

Borrowing.

Go to friends for advice;
To women for pity;
To strangers for charity;
To relatives for nothing.
Spanish Proverb.

I can get no remedy against this consumption of the purse; borrowing only lingers and lingers it out, but the disease is incurable. *Spanish Proverb.*

Bottle.

In the bottle, discontent seeks for comfort, cowardice for courage, and bashfulness for confidence. *Johnson.*

Bounty.

Such moderation with thy bounty join,
That thou may'st nothing give that is not
thine.
That liberality is but cast away,
Which makes us borrow what we cannot
pay. *Denham.*

Boxes.

The four boxes that rule the world—Cartridge-box, Ballot-box, Jury-box and Band-box.

Boyhood.

O! enviable, early days,
When dancing thoughtless pleasure's
mazes,
To care, to guilt unknown!
How ill exchang'd for riper times,
To feel the follies, or the crimes
Of others, or my own!
Ye tiny elves, that guiltless sport,

Like linnets in the bush,
Ye little know the ill ye court,
When manhood is your wish!
The losses, the crosses,
That active men engage;
The fears all, the tears all,
Of dim declining age.   *Burns.*

Ah! happy years! once more who would
not be a boy.   *Byron.*

Brains.

            Not Hercules
Could have knock'd out his brains, for he
    had none.   *Shakespeare.*

Bravery.

A spirit yet unquell'd and high,
That claims and seeks ascendency.
                    Byron.

A brave man may fall, but cannot yield.
A brave man may yield to a braver man.
None but the brave deserve the fair.
                    Dryden.

That's a valiant flea that dares eat his
breakfast on the lip of a lion.
                    Shakespeare.

He is not worthy of the honeycomb
That shuns the hive because the bees have
    stings.   *Shakespeare.*

The best hearts, Trim, are ever the bravest, replied my uncle Toby.   *Sterne.*
Nature often enshrines gallant and noble
hearts in weak bosoms—oftenest, God bless
her! in female breasts.   *Dickens.*

Breeding.

A well-bred dog generally bows to
strangers.

Brevity.

            Brevity is the soul of wit
And tediousness the outward limbs, and
    flourishes.   *Shakespeare.*

If you would be pungent, be brief; for
it is with words as with sunbeams—the
more they are condensed the deeper they
burn.   *Southey.*

37

Bribery.

Who thinketh to buy villainy with gold,
Shall ever find such faith so bought—so
    sold.   *Shakespeare.*

Silver, though white,
Yet it draws black lines; it shall not rule
    my palm
There to mark forth its base corruption,
       Middleton and Rowley.

Broken-Heart.

The heart will break, yet brokenly live on.
       Byron.

Brook.

Oh for a seat in some poetic nook
Just hid with trees and sparkling with a
    brook.   *Leigh Hunt.*

Building.

Never build after you are five and forty:
have five years' income in hand before you
lay a brick; and always calculate the expense at double the estimate.   *Kett.*

Bully.

A brave man is sometimes a desperado;
a bully is always a coward.   *Haliburton.*

Business.

A man who cannot mind his own business, is not to be trusted with the king's.
       Saville.

There are in business three things necessary—knowledge, temper and time.
       Feltham.

Never shrink from doing anything which
your business calls you to do. The man
who is above his business, may one day
find his business above him.   *Drew.*

But.

Oh, now comes that bitter word—but
Which makes all nothing that was **said**
    before,
That smooths and wounds, that strikes **and**
    dashes more
Than flat denial, or a plain disgrace.
       Daniel.

But yet

I do not like "but yet;" it does allay
The good precedence; fie upon "but yet;
"But yet" is as a jailer to bring forth
Some monstrous malefactor. *Shakespeare.*

Cake.

My cake is dough. *Shakespeare.*

Calamity.

How wisely fate ordain'd for human kind
Calamity! which is the perfect glass,
Wherein we truly see and know ourselves.
Davenant.

The willow which bends to the tempest.
often escapes better than the oak which
resists it; and so in great calamities, it
sometimes happens that light and frivol-
ous spirits recover their elasticity and presence of mind sooner than those of a
loftier character. *Sir Walter Scott.*

Calamity is man's true touchstone.
Beaumont and Fletcher.

Thus sometimes hath the brightest day a
cloud;
And, after summer, ever more succeeds
Barren winter with his wrathful nipping
cold,
So cares and joys abound, as seasons fleet.
Shakespeare.

Calm.

How calm,—how beautiful comes on
The stilly hour, when storms have gone,
When warring winds have died away
And clouds, beneath the dancing ray
Melt off and leave the land and sea,
Sleeping in bright tranquillity. *Moore.*

The tempest is o'er-blown, the skies are
clear,
And the sea charm'd into a calm so still
That not a wrinkle ruffles her smooth face.
Dryden.

Calumny.

False praise can please, and calumny af-
fright
None but the vicious, and the hypocrite.
Horace.

Be thou as chaste as ice, as pure as snow,
  thou
Shalt not escape calumny.   *Shakespeare.*

Candor.

        I hold it cowardice
To rest mistrustful where a noble heart
Hath pawn'd an open hand in sign of love.
                        Shakespeare.
The brave do never shun the light;
Just are their thoughts, and open are their
  tempers;
Truly without disguise they love and hate;
Still are they found in the fair face of day
And heav'n and men are judges of their
  actions.   *Rowe.*

  In simple and pure soul I come to you.
                        Shakespeare.

Cant.

'Tis too much prov'd—that, with devo-
  tion's visage
And pious action, we do sugar o'er
The devil himself.   *Shakespeare.*

Care.

Care keeps his watch in every old man's
  eye
And where care lodgeth, sleep will never
  lie.   *Shakespeare.*
Care is no cure, but rather a corrosive
For things that are not to be remedied.
                        Shakespeare.
Care seeks out wrinkled brows and hollow
  eyes,
And builds himself caves to abide in them.
                  Beaumont and Fletcher.
Still though the headlong cavalier,
O'er rough and smooth, in wild career,
    Seems racing with the wind;
His sad companion, ghastly pale,
And darksome as a widow's veil,
    Care keeps her seat behind.   *Horace.*
God tempers the wind to the shorn lamb.
                        Sterne.

Care that is once enter'd into the breast
Will have the whole possession ere it rest.
                        Johnson.

Man is a child of sorrow, and this world,
In which we breathe, has cares enough to
    plague us,
But it hath means withal to soothe these
    cares,
And he who meditates on others' woe,
Shall in that meditation lose his own.
                              Cumberland.

Cares.

Providence has given us *hope* and *sleep*,
. 3 a compensation for the many cares of
life.   *Voltaire.*

But human bodies are sic fools,
For a' their colleges and schools,
That when nae real ills perplex them,
They make enow themselves to vex them.
                              Burns.

Although my cares do hang upon my soul
Like mines of lead, the greatness of my
    spirit
Shall shake the sullen weight off.
                              Clapthorne.

Quick is the succession of human events:
the cares of to-day are seldom the cares of
to-morrow; and when we lie down at
night, we may safely say to most of our
troubles, "Ye have done your worst, and
we shall meet no more."   *Cowper.*

Cause.

A good cause makes a strong arm.

God befriend us, as our cause is just.
                              Shakespeare.

A noble cause doth ease much a griev-
ous case.   *Sir Philip Sidney.*

A rotten cause abides no handling.
                              Shakespeare.

Causes.

Small causes are sufficient to make a man
uneasy, when great ones are not in the
way; for want of a block he will stumble
at a straw.   *Swift.*

Caution.

It is a good thing to learn caution by the
misfortunes of others.   *Syrus.*

All's to be fear'd where all is to be lost.
Byron.

More firm and sure the hand of courage
    strikes,
When it obeys the watchful eye of caution.
Thomson.

                Trust none.
For oaths are straws, men's faiths are
    wafer cakes,
And hold-fast is the only dog.
Shakespeare

Beware equally of a sudden friend, and
a slow enemy.   *Home.*

Cautious Man.

He knows the compass, sail, and oar
Or never launches from the shore;
Before he builds computes the cost,
And in no proud pursuit is lost.   *Gay.*

Celibacy.

But earlier is the rose distill'd
Than that which withering on the virgin
    thorn
Grows, lives and dies in single blessedness.
Shakespeare.

Censure.

Horace appears in good humor while
he censures, and therefore his censure has
the more weight as supposed to proceed
from judgment, not from passion. *Young.*
The censure of those that are opposed
to us, is the nicest commendation that can
be given us.   *St. Evremond.*

Few persons have sufficient wisdom to
prefer censure which is useful to them, to
praise which deceives them.
La Rochefoucauld.

Ceremony.

Ceremony was but devis'd at first
To set a gloss on faint deeds—hollow wel-
    comes,
Recanting goodness, sorry e'er 'tis shown;
But where there is true friendship, there
    needs none.   *Shakespeare.*

All ceremonies are, in themselves, very silly things; but yet a man of the world should know them. They are the out-works of manners and decency, which would be too often broken in upon, if it were not for that defence, which keeps the enemy at a proper distance. It is for this reason that I always treat fools and coxcombs with great ceremony: true good breeding not being a sufficient barrier against them.   *Chesterfield.*

As ceremony is the invention of wise men to keep fools at a distance, so good breeding is an expedient to make fools and wise men equal.   *Steele.*

Chance.

A lucky chance that oft decides the fate
Of mighty monarchs.   *Thomson.*
Although men flatter themselves with their great actions, they are not so often the result of a great design as of chance.
                La Rochefoucauld.

As the ancients wisely say
Have a care o' th' main chance,
And look before you ere you leap;
For as you sow y'ere like to reap.
                Butler.
Be careful still of the main chance.
                Dryden.

Change.

Ships, wealth, general confidence,—
All were his;
He counted them at break of day,
And when the sun set! where were
   they?   *Byron.*
Gather ye rosebuds while ye may,
   Old Time is still a flying;
And that same flower that blooms to-day,
   To-morrow shall be dying.   *Herrick.*

Character.

Those who see thee in thy full blown
   pride,
Know little of affections crushed within
And wrongs which frenzy thee.
                Talfourd.

Thou wilt quarrel with a man that hath a hair more or a hair less in his beard than thou hast. Thou wilt quarrel with a man for cracking nuts, having no other reason but because thou hast hazel eyes; what eye but such an eye, would spy out such a quarrel? Thy head is as full of quarrels, as an egg is full of meat.

Shakespeare.

Those who quit their proper character to assume what does not belong to them, are for the greater part ignorant of both the character they leave and of the character they assume. *Burke.*

He who when called upon to speak a disagreeable truth, tells it boldly and has done, is both bolder and milder than he who nibbles in a low voice and never ceases nibbling. *Lavater.*

Decision of character is one of the most important of human qualities, philosophically considered. Speculation, knowledge, is not the chief end of man; it is action. * * * "Give us the man," shout the multitude, "who will step forward and take the responsibility." He is instantly the idol, the lord, and the king among men. He, then, who would command among his fellows, must excel them more in energy of will than in power of intellect. *Burnap.*

Character is a perfectly educated will. *Novalis.*

Spare in diet;
Free from gross passion, or of mirth, or anger;
Constant in spirit, not swerving with the blood;
Garnish'd and deck'd with modest compliment;
Not working with the eye, without the ear,
And, but purged in judgment, trusting neither. *Shakespeare.*

The best rules to form a young man are, to talk little, to hear much, to reflect alone upon what has passed in company, to distrust one's own opinions, and value others that deserve it. *Sir Wm. Temple.*

Best men are often moulded out of faults.
                              Shakespeare.

Every man has in himself a continent of
undiscovered character. Happy is he who
acts the Columbus to his own soul.
                              Sir J. Stevens.

The most trifling actions that affect a
man's credit are to be regarded.   The
sound of your hammer at five in the morning, or nine at night, heard by a creditor,
makes him easy six months longer; but if
he sees you at a Billiard table, or hears
your voice at a Tavern, when you should
be at work, he sends for his money the
next day.   *Franklin.*

Characters.

Nature hath fram'd strange bed-fellows in
    her time ;
Some, that will evermore peep through
    their eyes,
And laugh like parrots, at a bag-piper ;
And other of such vinegar aspect,
That they'll not show their teeth in way of
    smile
Though Nestor swear the jest be laughable.
                              Shakespeare.

Charity.

Charity suffereth long, and is kind ; charity envieth not ; charity vaunteth not itself,
is not puffed up, doth not behave itself
unseemly, seeketh not her own, is not
easily provoked, thinketh no evil ; rejoiceth
not in iniquity but rejoiceth in the truth ;
beareth all things, believeth all things,
hopeth all things, endureth all things.
                              1 Cor. xiii. 1.

And now abideth faith, hope and charity,
these three ; but the greatest of these is
charity.   *1 Cor.* xiii, 13.

Gently to hear, kindly to judge.
                              Shakespeare.

Give to him that asketh thee ; and from
him that would borrow of thee turn not
thou away.   *Matthew.*

Charity shall cover a multitude of sins.
                              1 Peter iv, 8.

He who receives a good turn should never forget it; he who does one should never remember it.   *Charron.*

The drying up a single tear has more
Of honest fame than shedding seas of gore.
                                                    Byron.

Charity ever
Finds in the act reward, and needs no trumpet
In the receiver.   *Beaumont and Fletcher.*

For true charity
Though ne'er so secret finds its just reward.   *May.*

A woman who wants a charitable heart, wants a pure mind.   *Haliburton.*

A physician is not angry at the intemperance of a mad patient, nor does he take it ill to be railed at by a man in a fever. Just so should a wise man treat all mankind, as a physician treats a patient, and look upon them only as sick and extravagant.   *Seneca.*

Chastity.

O, she is colder than the mountain's snow,
To such a subtile purity she's wrought.
                                                    Crown.

Chaste as the icicle
That's curdled by the frost of purest snow,
And hangs on Dian's temple.
                                            Shakespeare.

Cheerfulness.

Give us, O give us, the man who sings at his work! Be his occupation what it may, he is equal to any of those who follow the same pursuit in silent sullenness. He will do more in the same time—he will do it better—he will persevere longer.
                                                    Carlyle.

A merry heart goes all the day,
    A sad tires in a mile.   *Shakespeare.*
Cheerfulness is health; the opposite, melancholy, is disease.   *Haliburton.*

Child.

The child is father of the man.
                                            Wordsworth.

How sharper than a serpent's tooth it is
To have a thankless child.
Shakespeare.

Train up a child in the way he should go;
and when he is old he will not depart from
it.   *Proverbs* xxii, 6.

Childhood.

Sweet childish days that were as long
As twenty days are now.   *Wordsworth.*

A simple child,
That lightly draws its breath,
And feels its life in every limb,
What should it know of death?
Wordsworth.

Children.

Fragile beginnings of a mighty end.
Mrs. Norton.

Delightful task! to rear the tender
    thought,
To teach the young idea how to shoot,
To pour the fresh instruction o er the
    mind,
To breathe the enlivening spirit and to
    fix
The generous purpose in the glowing
    breast!   *Thomson.*

Call not that man wretched, who whatever ills he suffers, has a child to love.
Southey.

Choice.

When better cherries are not to be had,
We needs must take the seeming best of
    bad.   *Daniel.*

The measure of choosing well, is
whether a man likes what he has chosen.
Lamb.

There's a small choice in rotten apples.
Shakespeare.

Christ.

Jesus Christ the same yesterday, to-day,
and forever.   *Hebrews* xiii, 8.

The best of men
That e'er wore earth about Him was a
    sufferer,

A soft, meek, patient, humble, tranquil
    spirit,
The first true gentleman that ever
    breathed.   *Decker.*

Christian.

A christian in this world is but gold in
the ore; at death the pure gold is melted
out and separated and the dross cast away
and consumed.   *Flavel.*

A christian is the highest style of man.
    Young.

A christian is God Almighty's gentleman.   *J. C. Hare.*

Christianity.

Ours is a religion jealous in its de-
mands, but how infinitely prodigal in its
gifts! It troubles you for an hour, it re-
pays you by immortality.   *Bulwer.*

Church.

What is a church? Our honest sexton
    tells,
'Tis a tall building, with a tower and bells.
    Crabbe.

Look on this edifice of marble made—
How fair it swells, too beautiful to fade.
See what fine people in its portals crowd,
Smiling and greeting, talking, laughing
    loud!
What is it? Surely not a gay exchange,
Where wit and beauty social joys arrange,
Not a grand shop, where late Parisian
    styles
Attract rich buyers from a thousand
    miles?
But step within; no need of further
    search.
Behold, admire a fashionable church!
Look how its oriel window glints and
    gleams,
What tinted light magnificently streams
On the proud pulpit, carved with quaint
    device,
Where velvet cushions, exquisitely nice,
Presse'd by the polish'd preacher's dainty
    hands,

Hold a large volume clasp'd by golden
    bands.   *Park Benjamin.*

Ciphers.

There are foure great cyphers in the
world; hee that is lame among dancers,
dumbe among lawyers, dull among schol-
lars, and rude amongst courtiers.
                  Bishop Earle.

Civility.

Whilst thou livest keep a good tongue in
thy head.   *Shakespeare.*

A good word is an easy obligation, but
not to speak ill, requires only our silence,
which costs us nothing.   *Tillotson.*

The insolent civility of a proud man is,
if possible, more shocking than his rude-
ness could be; because he shows you, by
his manner, that he thinks it mere conde-
scension in him; and that his goodness
alone bestows upon you what you have no
pretense to claim.   *Chesterfield.*

Cleanliness.

Even from the body's purity, the mind
Receives a secret, sympathetic aid.
                  Thomson.

Let thy mind's sweetness have its operation upon thy body, clothes, and habitation.   *Herbert.*

Clock.

A clock! with its ponderous embowel-
ments of lead and brass, its pert or solemn
dullness of communication.   *Lamb.*

Clouds.

Was I deceived, or did a sable cloud
Turn forth her silver lining on the night?
                  Milton.

Those playful fancies of the mighty sky.
                  Smith.

That look'd
As though an angel, in his upward flight,
Had left his mantle floating in mid-air.
            Joanna Baillie.

49

Cock.

I have heard
The cock, that is the trumpet to the morn,
Doth, with his lofty and shrill-sounding
throat,
Awake the god of day.   *Shakespeare.*

Coffee.

Coffee, which makes the politician wise,
And see through all things with his half
shut eyes.   *Pope.*

Comfort.

Sweet as refreshing dews or summer
showers,
To the long parching thirst of drooping
flowers ;
Grateful as fanning gales to fainting
swains
And soft as trickling balm to bleeding
pains.
Such are thy words.   *Gay.*
I would bring balm and pour it into your
wound,
Cure your distemper'd mind and heal your
fortunes.   *Dryden.*
Thy words have darted hope into my soul
And comfort dawns upon me. *Southern.*

Commander.

It is better to have a lion at the head of
an army of sheep, than a sheep at the head
of an army of lions.   *Defoe.*

Commendation.

Commend a fool for his wit, or a knave
for his honesty, and they will receive you
into their bosom.   *Fielding.*

Commerce.

A well regulated commerce is not, like
law. physic, or divinity, to be overstocked
with hands : but, on the contrary, flour-
ishes by multitudes, and gives employment
to all its professors.   *Addison.*

Companions.

The most agreeable of all companions is a simple, frank man, without any high pretensions to an oppressive greatness; one who loves life, and understands the use of it; obliging, alike at all hours; above all, of a golden temper, and steadfast as an anchor. For such an one we gladly exchange the great genius, the most brilliant wit, the profoundest thinker. *Lessing*.

Company.

No company is far preferable to bad, because we are more apt to catch the vices of others than virtues, as disease is far more courageous than health. *Colton*.

Bad company is like a nail driven into a post, which, after the first or second blow, may be drawn out with little difficulty; but being once driven up to the head, the pincers cannot take hold to draw it out, but which can only be done by the destruction of the wood. *Augustine*.

Take rather than give the tone to the company you are in. If you have parts you will show them more or less upon every subject; and if you have not, you had better talk sillily upon a subject of other people's than of your own choosing. *Chesterfield*.

No man can possibly improve in any company for which he has not respect enough to be under some degree of restraint. *Chesterfield*.

Compensation.

When articles rise the consumer is the first that suffers, and when they fall, he is the last that gains. *Colton*.

Competence.

O grant me, heav'n, a middle state
Neither too humble or too great;
More than enough for nature's ends,
With something left to treat my friends.
Mallet.

Complaining.

I will not be as those who spend the day in complaining of the head-ache, and the night in drinking the wine that gives the head-ache.   *Goethe.*

Compliments.

Compliments of congratulation are always kindly taken, and cost nothing but pen, ink and paper. I consider them as draughts upon good breeding, where the exchange is always greatly in favor of the drawer.   *Chesterfield.*

Concealment.

We shall find that it is less difficult to hide a thousand guineas than one hole in your coat.   *Colton.*

To conceal anything from those to whom I am attached, is not in my nature. I can never close my lips where I have opened my heart.   *Dickens.*

Conceit.

Conceit is to nature what paint is to beauty; it is not only needless, but impairs what it would improve.   *Pope.*

A strong conceit is rich; so most men
          deem;
If not to be, 'tis comfort yet to seem.
          Marston.

The more any one speaks of himself, the less he likes to hear another talked of.
          Lavater.

Conceit in weakest bodies strongest works.
          Shakespeare.

Conceit and Confidence.

Success seems to be that which forms the distinction between confidence and conceit. Nelson, when young was piqued at not being noticed in a certain paragraph of the newspapers, which detailed an action wherein he had assisted "But never mind," said he, "I will one day have a gazette of my own."   *Colton.*

Conciliation.

Agree with thine adversary quickly while thou art in the way with him.
Matt. v, 25.

Conclusion.

O most lame and impotent conclusion.
Shakespeare.

Conduct.

Have more than thou showest,
Speak less than thou knowest,
Lend less than thou owest,
Learn more than thou trowest,
Set less than thou throwest.
Shakespeare.

Confession.

A man should never be ashamed to own he has been in the wrong, which is but saying, in other words, that he is wiser today than he was yesterday. *Pope.*

Confidence.

There is a kind of greatness which does not depend upon fortune; it is a certain manner that distinguishes us, and which seems to destine us for great things; it is the value we insensibly set upon ourselves; it is by this quality, that we gain the deference of other men, and it is this which commonly raises us more above them, than birth, rank, or even merit itself.
La Rochefoucauld.

Confusion.

Confusion now hath made his masterpiece!
Shakespeare.

With ruin upon ruin, rout on rout,
Confusion worse confounded. *Milton.*

Conscience.

Suspicion haunts the guilty mind
The thief doth fear each bush an officer.
Shakespeare.

I feel within me
A peace above all earthly dignities,
A still and quiet conscience.
Shakespeare.

The torture of a bad conscience is the hell of a living soul.　*Calvin.*

What stronger breast-plate than a heart untainted?
Thrice is he arm'd, who hath his quarrel just;
And he but naked, though lock'd up in steel,
Whose conscience with injustice is corrupted.　*Shakespeare.*

My conscience hath a thousand several tongues,
And every tongue brings in a several tale;
And every tale condemns me for a villain.
　　　Shakespeare.

Man's conscience is the oracle of God!
　　　Byron.

Conscience has no more to do with gallantry than it has with politics.　*Sheridan.*

Thus conscience doth make cowards of us all.　*Shakespeare.*

A still, small voice.　*1 Kings* xix, 12.

Consequences.

As the dimensions of the tree are not always regulated by the size of the seed, so the consequences of things are not always proportionate to the apparent magnitude of those events that have produced them.
　　　Colton.

Consistency.

Either take Christ in your lives, or cast him out of your lips; either be that thou seemest, or else be what thou art.　*Dyer.*

Conspiracies.

Conspiracies no sooner should be form'd
Than executed.　*Addison.*

Constancy.

There are two kinds of constancy in love, one arising from incessantly finding in the loved one fresh objects to love, the other from regarding it as a point of honor to be constant.
　　　La Rochefoucauld.

I am constant as the northern star;
Of whose true fix'd and resting quality
There is no fellow in the firmament.
Shakespeare.

Contemplation.

There is no lasting pleasure but contemplation; all others grow flat and insipid upon frequent use; and when a man hath run through a set of vanities, in the declension of his age, he knows not what to do with himself, if he cannot think; he saunters about from one dull business to another, to wear out time; and hath no reason to value Life but because he is afraid of death.   *Burnet.*

Contempt.

Those only are despicable who fear to be despised.   *La Rochefoucauld.*

Despise not any man, and do not spurn any thing. For there is no man that hath not his hour, nor is there any thing that hath not its place.   *Rabbi Ben Azai.*

Content.

There is a jewel which no Indian mine can
        buy,
No chemic art can counterfeit;
It makes men rich in greatest poverty,
Makes water wine, turns wooden cups to
        gold,
The homely whistle to sweet music's
        strain;
Seldom it comes to few from Heaven sent,
That much in little—all in naught—*content.*   *Wilbye.*

Poor and content is rich and rich enough;
But riches, fineless, is as poor as winter,
To him that ever fears he shall be poor.
Shakespeare.

Contentment.

Contentment, rosy, dimpled maid,
Thou brightest daughter of the sky.
Lady Manners.

Contentment, parent of delight.   *Green.*

55

Contentment produces in some measure, all those effects which the alchymist usually ascribes to what he calls the philosopher's stone; and if it does not bring riches, it does the same thing, by banishing the desire of them. If it cannot remove the disquietudes arising from a man's mind, body, or fortune, it makes him easy under them. *Addison.*

Happy the man who void of care and
    strife,
In silken or in leather purse retains
A good old shilling. *Goldsmith.*

As for a little more money and a little more time, why it's ten to one, if either one or the other would make you one whit happier. If you had more time, it would be sure to hang heavily. It is the working man who is the happy man. Man was made to be active, and he is never so happy as when he is so. It is the idle man who is the miserable man. What comes of holidays, and far too often of sight-seeing, but evil? Half the harm that happens is on these days. And, as for money—Don't you remember the old saying, "Enough is as good as a feast"? Money never made a man happy yet, nor will it. There is nothing in its nature to produce happiness. The more a man has, the more he wants. Instead of its filling a vacuum, it makes one. If it satisfies one want, it doubles and trebles that want another way. That was a true proverb of the wise man, rely upon it: "Better is little with the fear of the Lord, than great treasure, and trouble therewith." *Franklin.*

Contiguity.

Speaking generally, no man appears great to his contemporaries, for the same reason that no man is great to his servants—both know too much of him. *Colton.*

Conversation.

Speak little and well, if you wish to be considered as possessing merit. *From the French.*

It is a secret known to but few, yet of no small use in the conduct of life, that when you fall into a man's conversation, the first thing you should consider is, whether he has a greater inclination to hear you, or that you should hear him.

Steele.

The fullest instruction, and the fullest enjoyment are never derived from books, till we have ventilated the ideas thus obtained, in free and easy chat with others.

Wm. Matthews.

Talking is a digestive process which is absolutely essential to the mental constitution of the man who devours many books. A full mind must have talk, or it will grow dyspeptic.

Wm. Matthews.

The first ingredient in conversation is truth, the next, good sense, the third, good humor, and the fourth, wit.

Sir Wm. Temple.

He who sedulously attends, pointedly asks, calmly speaks, coolly answers, and ceases when he has no more to say, is in possession of some of the best requisites of man.

Lavater.

Converser.

He is so full of pleasant anecdote;
So rich, so gay, so poignant in his wit,
Time vanishes before him as he speaks,
And ruddy morning through the lattice peeps
Ere night seems well begun.

Joanna Baillie.

Coquette.

There affectation, with a sickly mein,
Shows in her cheeks the roses of eighteen,
Practis'd to lisp and hang the head aside,
Faints into airs and languishes with pride;
On the rich quilt sinks with becoming woe,
Wrapt in a gown for sickness and for show.

Pope.

57

See how the world its veterans rewards!
A youth of frolics, an old age of cards;
Fair to no purpose, artful to no end,
Young without lovers, old without a
    friend;
A fop their passion but their prize a sot,
Alive ridiculous, and dead forgot!   *Pope.*

   The vain coquette each suit disdains,
    And glories in her lover's pains;
   With age she fades—each lover flies.
   Contemn'd, forlorn, she pines and dies.
                       Gay.

Corpulence.

Let me have men about me that are fat,
Sleek-headed men and such as sleep
    o'nights.
Yond' Cassius has a lean and hungry look;
He thinks too much; such men are dan-
    gerous.   *Shakespeare.*

   Still she strains the aching clasp
    That binds her virgin zone;
   I know it hurts her, though she looks
    As cheerful as she can.
   Her waist is larger than her life
   For life is but a span.   *Holmes.*

Corruption.

E'en grave divines submit to glittering
    gold,
The best of consciences are bought and
    sold.   *Dr. Wolcot.*

Countenance.

   The countenance may be rightly defined
as the title page which heralds the con-
tents of the human volume, but like other
title pages, it sometimes puzzles, often
misleads, and often says nothing to the
purpose.   *Wm. Matthews.*

   Physically, they exhibited no indication
of their past lives and characters. The
greatest scamp had a Raphael face, with
a profusion of blonde hair; Oakhurst, a
gambler, had the melancholy character
and intellectual abstraction of a Hamlet;
the coolest and most courageous man was
scarcely over five feet in height, with a
soft voice, and an embarrassed manner.
                      Bret Harte

The cheek
Is apter than the tongue to tell an errand.
Shakespeare.

A countenance more
In sorrow than in anger.
Shakespeare.

Country.

Scenes must be beautiful which daily
view'd
Please daily, and whose novelty survives
Long knowledge and the scrutiny of years.
Cowper.

God made the country and man made the
town ;
What wonder then, that health and virtue,
gifts
That can alone make sweet the bitter
draught
That life holds out to all, should most
abound,
And least be threaten'd in the fields and
groves? *Cowper.*

And see the country, far diffused around,
One boundless blush, one white impurpled
shower
Of mingled blossoms ; where the raptured
eye
Hurries from joy to joy. *Thomson.*

He who loves not his country can love
nothing. *Johnson.*

And lives there a man, with soul so dead
Who never to himself hath said—
This is my own, my native land ! *Scott.*

Had I a dozen sons, each in my love
alike, I had rather have eleven die nobly
for their country, than one voluptuously
surfeit out of action. *Shakespeare.*

Country Life.

Here too dwells simple truth ; plain inno-
cence ;
Unsullied beauty ; sound unbroken youth,
Patient of labor, with a little pleas'd ;
Health ever blooming ; unambitious toil,
Calm contemplation ; and poetic ease.
Thomson.

59

How various his employments, whom the
    world
Calls idle, and who justly in return
Esteems that busy world an idler too!
Friends, books, a garden, and perhaps his
    pen,
Delightful industry enjoyed at home,
And nature in her cultivated trim,
Dressed to his taste, inviting him abroad.
Cowper.

Courage.

Courage consists not in blindly over-
looking danger, but in seeing it, and conquering it. *Richter.*

The intent and not the deed
Is in our power; and, therefore, who dares
    greatly,
Does greatly. *Brown.*

Most men have more courage than even
they themselves think they have.
Greville.

The smallest worm will turn, being trod-
    den on;
And doves will peck, in safeguard of their
    brood. *Shakespeare.*

I do not think a braver gentleman,
More active-valiant, or more valiant
    young,
More daring, or more bold, is now alive,
To grace this latter age with noble deeds.
Shakespeare.

True courage scorns
To vent her prowess in a storm of words,
And to the valiant action speaks alone.
Smollett.

Prithee peace:
I dare do all that may become a man,
Who dares do more is none.
Shakespeare.

Rocks have been shaken from their solid
    base,
But what shall move a firm and dauntless
    mind? *Joanna Baillie.*

Courtesy.

Ill seemes (say'd he) if he so valiant be,
That he should be so sterne to stranger
  wight;
For seldom yet did living creature see
That courtesie and manhood ever disagree.
       Spenser.

As the sword of the best-tempered
metal is the most flexible; so the truly
generous are most pliant and courteous
in their behavior to their inferiors.
       Fuller.

Courtiers.

A toad-eater's an imp I don't admire.
       Dr. Wolcot.

I am no courtier, no fawning dog of state,
To lick and kiss the hand that buffets me;
Nor can I smile upon my guest and praise
His stomach, when I know he feeds on
  poison,
And death disguised sits grinning at my
  table.   *Sewell.*

   A mere court butterfly,
That flutters in the pageant of a monarch.
       Byron.

Courtship.

There is, sir, a critical minute in
Ev'ry man's wooing, when his mistress
  may
Be won, which if he carelessly neglect
To prosecute, he may wait long enough
Before he gain the like opportunity.
     Marmion's Antiquary.

Men are April when they woo, December when they wed, and maids are May
when they are maids, but the sky changes
when they are wives.   *Shakespeare.*

  Women are angels wooing;
Things won are done, joy's soul lies in the
  doing;
That she belov'd knows nought, that knows
  not this,—
Men prize the thing ungain'd more than it
  is.   *Shakespeare.*

Courtship consists in a number of quiet
attentions, not so pointed as to alarm,
nor so vague as not to be understood.

Sterne.

Say that she rail; why then I'll tell her
plain,
She sings as sweetly as a nightingale;
Say that she frown; I'll say she looks as
clear
As morning roses, newly wash'd with
dew;
Say she be mute and will not speak a
word,
Then I'll commend her volubility
And say she uttereth piercing eloquence.

Shakespeare.

Trust me—with women worth the being
won,
The softest lover ever best succeeds.

Hill.

That man that hath a tongue I say is no
man,
Win her with gifts if she respect not
words;
Dumb jewels often in their silent kind,
More quick than words do move a woman's
mind. *Shakespeare.*

If with his tongue he cannot win a woman. *Shakespeare.*

She is a woman, therefore may be woo'd,
She is a woman, therefore may be won.

Shakespeare.

Covetousness.

We never desire earnestly what we desire in reason. *La Rochefoucauld.*

He deservedly loses his own property,
who covets that of another. *Phoedrus.*

The things which belong to others please
us more, and that which is ours, is more
pleasing to others. *Syrus.*

Coward.

Bold at the council board
But cautious in the field. *Dryden.*

A coward; a most devout; religious in it.
Shakespeare.

I know him a notorious liar,
Think him a great way fool, solely a coward.   *Shakespeare.*

Go—let thy less than woman's hand
Assume the distaff—not the brand.
                              Byron.

Cowards fear to die; but courage stout,
Rather than live in snuff, will be put out.
                    Sir Walter Raleigh.
Cowards die many times before their
deaths;
The valiant never taste of death but once.
                         Shakespeare.

Cowardice.

Those that fly may fight again,
Which he can never do that's slain,
Hence timely running's no mean part
Of conduct in the martial art.   *Butler.*

Creation.

The heavens declare the glory of God,
and the firmament showeth his handiwork.
Day unto day uttereth speech, and night
unto night showeth knowledge. There is
no speech nor language where their voice
is not heard.   *Psalms* xix, 1.

The spacious firmament on high,
With all the blue ethereal sky,
And spangled heavens, a shining frame
Their great Original proclaim.

*   *   *   *   *   *

Forever singing as they shine
The hand that made us is divine.
                            Addison.

Creditor.

The creditor whose appearance gladdens
the heart of a debtor, may hold his head
in sunbeams and his foot on storms.
                            Lavater.

Creditors.

Creditors have better memories than
debtors; and Creditors are a superstitious
sect, great observers of set days and times.
                            Franklin.

Crime.

One crime is concealed by the commis-
sion of another.   *Seneca.*

Where have you ever found that man
who stopped short after the perpetration
of a single crime? *Juvenal.*

For he that but conceives a crime in
  thought,
Contracts the danger of an actual fault.
Creech.

Every crime
Has, in the moment of its perpetration,
Its own avenging angel—dark misgiving,
An ominous sinking at the inmost heart.
Coleridge.

Criticism.

Criticism is like champagne, nothing
more execrable if bad, nothing more excellent if good; if meagre, muddy, vapid,
and sour, both are fit only to engender
colic and wind; but if rich, generous and
sparkling, they communicate a glow to
the spirits, improve the taste, expand the
heart, and are worthy of being introduced
at the symposium of the gods. *Colton.*

Damn with faint praise, assent with civil
  leer,
And without sneering, teach the rest to
  sneer;
Willing to wound, and yet afraid to strike,
Just hint a fault, and hesitate dislike.
Pope.

Get your enemies to read your works in
order to mend them, for your friend is so
much your second selve that he will judge
too like you. *Pope.*

Critics.

Critics are a kind of freebooters in the
republic of letters,—who like deer, goats
and divers other gramniverous animals,
gain subsistence by gorging upon buds
and leaves of the young shrubs of the
forest, thereby robbing them of their verdure, and retarding their progress to ma-
turity. *Washington Irving.*

A poet that fails in writing, becomes
often a morose critic. The weak and insipid white wine makes at length excellent
vinegar. *Shenstone.*

Crown.

Uneasy lies the head that wears a crown.
Shakespeare.

Cruelty.

I would not enter in my list of friends,
(Though grac'd with polish'd manners and
    fine sense,
Yet wanting sensibility), the man
Who needlessly sets foot upon a worm.
An inadvertent step may crush the snail
That crawls at evening in the public path,
But he that has humanity, forwarn'd,
Will tread aside, and let the reptile live.
Cowper.

Cunning.

Cunning and treachery are the offspring
of incapacity. *La Rochefoucauld.*
It is sometimes necessary to play the
fool to avoid being deceived by cunning
men. *La Rochefoucauld.*

Cunning and Wisdom.

We take cunning for a sinister and
crooked wisdom, and certainly there is a
great difference between a cunning man
and a wise man, not only in point of honesty but in point of ability. *Bacon.*

Curiosity.

Inquisitive people are the funnels of
conversation; they do not take in anything
for their own use, but merely to pass it to
another. *Steele.*

I loathe that low vice curiosity.
Byron.

Cursing.

This nor hurts him, nor profits you a jot:
Forbear it, therefore; give your cause to
    heaven. *Shakespeare.*

Custom.

Custom is the law of fools. *Vanburgh.*

Custom does often reason overrule
And only serves for reason to the fool.
Rochester.

Custom, 'tis true, a venerable tyrant
O'er servile man extends her blind do-
    minion. *Thomson.*

Dancing.

Dear creature! you'd swear
When her delicate feet in the dance twin-
    kle round,
That her steps are of light, that her home
    is the air,
And she only "par complaisance" touches
    the ground.   *Moore.*

    Her feet beneath her petticoat,
    Like little mice, stole in and out,
      As if they feared the light.
    And oh! she dances such a way,
    No sun upon an Easter day
      Is half so fine a sight.   *Suckling.*

    Come, trip it as you go,
    On the light fantastic toe.   *Milton.*

Danger.

For danger levels man and brute
And all are fellows in their need.
                   Dryden.

Darkness.

How sweetly did they float upon the wings
Of silence, through the empty-vaulted
    night,
At every fall smoothing the raven-down
Of darkness till it smiled.   *Milton.*

Dark night that from the eye his function
    takes,
The ear more quick of apprehension
    makes,
Wherein it doth impair the seeing sense,
It pays the hearing double recompense.
             Shakespeare.

Day.

One of the heavenly days that cannot die.
             Wordsworth.

"I've lost a day"—the prince who nobly
    cried
Had been an emperor, without his crown.
                Young.

Daybreak.

At last the golden oriental gate
Of greatest heaven 'gan to open fair;
And Phœbus, fresh as bridegroom to his
    mate,
Came dancing forth shaking his dewy hair,

And hurl'd his glist'ning beams through
    gloomy air.   *Spenser.*

It was a lark, the herald of the morn,
No nightingale; look love, what envious
    streaks
Do lace the severing clouds in yonder
    east;
Night's candles are burnt out, and jocund
    day
Stands tip-toe on the misty mountain tops.
    Shakespeare.

Dead.

Weep not for him that dieth,
    For he hath ceased from tears,
And a voice to his replieth
    Which he hath not heard for years.
    Mrs. Norton.

All that tread
The globe are but a handful to the tribes
That slumber in its bosom.   Take the
    wings
Of morning, and the Barcan desert pierce,
Or lose thyself in the continuous woods
Where rolls the Oregon, and hears no
    sound
Save his own dashings,—yet the dead are
    there;
And millions in those solitudes, since first
The flight of years began, have laid them
    down
In their last sleep; the dead reign there
    alone.   *Bryant.*

Duncan is in his grave;
After life's fitful fever he sleeps well;
Treason has done his worst; nor steel, nor
    poison,
Malice domestic, foreign levy, nothing
Can touch him further.   *Shakespeare.*

Death.

O death! the poor man's dearest friend,
    The kindest and the best!
Welcome the hour, my aged limbs
    Are laid with thee at rest!   *Burns.*

Let no man fear to die, we love to sleep
    all,
And death is but the sounder sleep.
    Beaumont.

To what base uses may we return!
Why may not imagination trace the noble
dust of Alexander, till it find it stopping
a bunghole? As thus: Alexander died,
Alexander was buried, Alexander return-
eth to dust; the dust is earth: of earth
we make loam. And why of that loam,
whereto he was converted, might they
not stop a beer barrel?

Shakespeare.

But yesterday the word of Cæsar might
Have stood against the world; now lies he
    there,
And none so poor to do him reverence.

Shakespeare.

Death opens the gate of fame, and shuts
the gate of envy after it; it unlooses the
chain of the captive, and puts the bonds-
man's task into another man's hand.

Sterne.

O grave! where is thy victory?
O death! where is thy sting? *Pope.*

Whom the Gods love die young.

Byron.

Why, what is pomp, rule, reign, but earth
    and dust?
And live we how we can, yet die we must.

Shakespeare.

And thou art terrible—the tear,
The groan, the knell, the pall, the bier;
And all we know, or dream, or fear
Of agony, are thine. *Halleck.*

Nothing in his life
Became him like the leaving it; he died
As one who had been studied in his death,
To throw away the dearest thing he owed,
As 'twere a careless trifle. *Shakespeare.*

Weep not for those
Who sink within the arms of death
Ere yet the chilling wintry breath
    Of sorrow o'er them blows;
But weep for them who here remain,
The mournful heritors of pain,
Condemn'd to see each bright joy fade,
And mark grief's melancholy shade
    Flung o'er Hope's fairest rose.

Mrs. Embury.

If I must die
I will encounter darkness as a bride
And hug it in my arms.   *Shakespeare.*

It is hard
To feel the hand of death arrest one's
  steps,
Throw a chill blight o'er all one's budding
  hopes,
And hurl one's soul untimely to the
  shades
Lost in the gaping gulf of blank oblivion.
                        Kirk White.

Death is but what the haughty brave,
The weak must bear, the wretch must
  crave.   *Byron.*

O death all eloquent, you only prcve
What dust we dote on, when 'tis man we
  love.   *Pope.*

Neither the sun nor death can be looked
at steadily.   *La Rochefoucauld.*

To die—to sleep—
No more;—and, by a sleep, to say we
  end
The heart-ache, and the thousand natural
  shocks,
That flesh is heir to,—'Tis a consumma-
  tion
Devoutly to be wish'd.   *Shakespeare.*

Leaves have their time to fall,
  And flowers to wither at the north
    wind's breath,
And stars to set; but all—
  Thou hast all seasons for thine own, O,
    death!   *Mrs. Hemans.*

Lay her i' the earth;
And from her fair and unpolluted flesh
May violets spring!   *Shakespeare.*
Oh my love, my wife!
Death, that hath suckt the honey of thy
  breath,
Hath had no power yet upon thy beauty,
Thou art not conquer'd; beauty's ensign
  yet
Is crimson in thy lips, and in thy cheeks,
And death's pale flag is not advanced
  there.
Why art thou yet so fair?   *Shakesbeare.*

Pale death approaches with an equal step, and knocks indiscriminately at the door of the cottage, and the portals of the palace.   *Horace.*

Death's but a path that *must* be trod,
If man would ever pass to God.
                                   Parnell.

It is impossible that anything so natural, so necessary, and so universal as death, should ever have been designed by Providence as an evil to mankind.   *Swift.*

For good men but *see* death, the wicked taste it.   *Johnson.*

Death is a commingling of eternity with time; in the death of a good man, eternity is seen looking through time.
                                   Goethe.

Thou know'st 'tis common; all that live
          must die,
Passing through nature to eternity.
                              Shakespeare.

Early, bright, transient
Chaste as morning dew
She parkled, was exhaled,
And went to heaven.   *Young.*

So live, that when thy summons comes to
          join
That innumerable caravan that moves
To that mysterious realm, where each
          shall take
His chamber in the silent halls of death,
Thou go not like the quarry-slave at night,
Scourged to his dungeon; but sustain'd
          and sooth'd
By an unfaltering trust, approach thy
          grave,
Like one that draws the drapery of his
          couch
Around him, and lies down to pleasant
          dreams.   *Bryant.*

All was ended now, the hope, the fear and
          the sorrow,
All the aching of heart, the restless, un-
          satisfied longing,
All the dull, deep pain, and constant an-
          guish of patience!   *Longfellow.*

A sleep without dreams, after a rough day
Of toil, is what we covet most; and yet
How clay shrinks back from mere quies-
    cent clay.   *Byron.*

It is not strange that that early love of
the heart should come back, as it so often
does when the dim eye is brightening with
its last light.   It is not strange that the
freshest fountains the heart has ever
known in its wastes should bubble up anew
when the life-blood is growing stagnant.
It is not strange that a bright memory
should come to a dying old man, as the
sunshine breaks across the hills at the
close of a stormy day; nor that in the
light of that ray, the very clouds that
made the day dark should grow gloriously
beautiful.   *Hawthorne.*

How wonderful is death!
Death and his brother sleep.
             Shelley.

Debt.

Run not into debt, either for wares
sold, or money borrowed; be content to
want things that are not of absolute
necessity, rather than run up the score.
          Sir M. Hale.

A public debt is a kind of anchor in the
storm; but if the anchor be too heavy for
the vessel, she will be sunk by that very
weight which was intended for her preser-
vation.   *Colton.*

Debtor.

The ghost of many a veteran bill
Shall hover around his slumbers.
            Holmes.

The ghostly dun shall worry his sleep,
  And constables cluster around him,
And he shall creep from the wood-hole
    deep.
Where their spectre eyes have found
    him.   *Holmes.*

Decay.

My way of life
Is fall'n into the sear and yellow leaf.
       Shakespeare.

Deceit.

Smooth runs the water, where the brook is
    deep;
And in his simple show he harbors trea-
    son.
The fox barks not when he would steal
    the lamb.   *Shakespeare.*

Decency.

Immodest words admit of no defence
For want of decency is want of sense.
        Earl of Roscommon.

Deception.

Of all the agonies of life, that which is
most poignant and harrowing—that which
for the time annihilates reason and leaves
our whole organization one lacerated,
mangled heart—is the conviction that we
have been deceived where we placed all
the trust of love.   *Bulwer.*

No man was ever so much deceived by
another as by himself.   *Greville.*

The first and worst of all frauds is to
cheat oneself. All sin is easy after that.
        Bailey.

Defects.

If we had no defects ourselves, we
should not take so much pleasure in not-
ing those of others.
        La Rochefoucauld.

In the intercourse of life we please,
often, more by our defects than by our
good qualities.   *La Rochefoucauld.*

Deformity.

Deformity of the heart I call
The worst deformity of all;
For what is form, or what is face.
But the soul's index, or its case?
        Colton.

Degeneracy.

What a falling off was there.
        Shakespeare.

Dejection.

Ah, there are moments for us here, when
    seeing
Life's inequalities, and woe, and care,
The burdens laid upon our mortal being
    Seem heavier than the human heart can
    bear.   *Phoebe Cary.*

Delays.

Be wise to-day, 'tis madness to defer
Next day, the fatal precedent will plead
Thus on, till wisdom is push'd out of life.
    Young.

Delicacy.

If you destroy delicacy and a sense of
shame in a young girl, you deprave her
very fast.   *Mrs. Stowe.*

Dependence.

There is none made so great, but he may
both need the help and service, and stand
in fear of the power and unkindness, even
of the meanest of mortals.   *Seneca.*

Depend on no man, on no friend, but
him who can depend on himself. He only
who acts conscientiously towards himself
will act so towards others, and vice versa.
    Lavater.

Desire.

O, fierce desire, the spring of sighs and
    tears,
    Reliev'd with want, impoverish'd with
    store,
Nurst with vain hopes, and fed with doubt-
    ful fears,
    Whose force withstood, increaseth more
    and more!   *Brandon.*

The desire of the moth for the star—
    Of the night for the morrow—
The devotion to something afar
    From the sphere of our sorrow.
    Shelley.

The passions and desires, like the two
twists of a rope, mutually mix one with
the other, and twine inextricably round
the heart; producing good if moderately
indulged; but certain destruction, if suffered to become inordinate.   *Burton.*

Desolation.

Such a house broke!
So noble a master fallen? all gone! and
  not
One friend to take his fortune by the arm,
And go along with him.
Shakespeare.

What is the worst of woes that wait on
  age?
What stamps the wrinkle deeper on the
  brow?
To view each lov'd one blotted from life's
  page,
And be alone on earth as I am now.
Byron.

Despair.

To doubt
Is worse than to have lost; And to de-
  spair
Is but to antedate those miseries
That must fall on us. *Massinger.*

He that despairs, degrades the Deity,
and seems to intimate, that He is insuf-
ficient, or not just to his word; and in
vain hath read the Scriptures, the world.
and man. *Feltham.*

Spirits of peace, where are ye? Are ye all
  gone?
And leave me here in wretchedness behind ye? *Shakespeare.*

Beware of desperate steps!—the darkest
  day
Live till to-morrow, will have passed away.
Cowper.

'Tis late before
The brave despair. *Thomson.*

Talk not of comfort, 'tis for lighter ills;
I will indulge my sorrows, and give way
To all the pangs and fury of despair.
Addison.

Despondency.

My heart is very tired—my strength is
  low—
My hands are full of blossoms pluck'd before
Held dead within them till myself shall
  die. *Mrs. Browning.*

Despots.

Despots govern by terror. They know that he who fears God fears nothing else; and, therefore, they eradicate from the mind, through their Voltaire, the Helœtius, and the rest of that infamous gang, that only sort of fear which generates true courage. *Burke.*

Destiny.

The wheels of nature are not made to roll backward; everything presses on toward Eternity; from the birth of Time an impetuous current has set in, which bears all the sons of men toward that interminable ocean. Meanwhile Heaven is attracting to itself whatever is congenial to its nature, is enriching itself by the spoils of earth, and collecting within its capacious bosom, whatever is pure, permanent and divine.
Robert Hall.

Destruction.

The gates of hell are open night and day;
Smooth the descent, and easy is the way;
But to return, and view the cheerful skies,
In this the task and mighty labor lies.
Dryden.

Determination.

I'll speak to it though hell itself should gape,
And bid me' hold my peace. *Shakespeare.*

Devotion.

Private devotions and secret offices of religion are like the refreshing of a garden with the distilling and petty drops of a water-pot; but, addressed from the temple, are like rain from heaven.
Jeremy Taylor.

Dew.

As fresh as morning dew distill'd on lowers. *Shakespeare.*
I must go seek some dew-drops here,
And hang a pearl in every cowslip's ear.
Shakespeare.

The starlight dews
All silently their tears of love instil
Weeping themselves away, till they in-
fuse
Deep into nature's breast, the spirit of her
hues.   *Byron.*

Diet.

All courageous animals are carnivorous,
and greater courage is to be expected in a
people, such as the English, whose food is
strong and hearty, than in the half starved
commonalty of other countries.
                          Sir W. Temple.

Simple diet is best;—for many dishes
bring many diseases; and rich sauces are
worse than even heaping several meats
upon each other.   *Pliny.*

Differences.

In differing breasts what differing passions
glow!
Ours kindle quick, but yours extinguish
slow.   *Garth.*

Difficulty.

Difficulty is a severe instructor, set over
us by the supreme ordinance of a parental
guardian and legislator, who knows us better than we know ourselves; and He loves
us better too. He that wrestles with us
strengthens our nerves, and sharpens our
skill. Our antagonist is our helper. This
amicable conflict with difficulty obliges us
to an intimate acquaintance with our object, and compels us to consider it in all
its relations. It will not suffer us to be
superficial.   *Burke.*

Digestion.

A light supper, a good night's sleep and
a fine morning have often made a hero of
the same man, who, by indigestion, a restless night and a rainy morning would
have proved a coward.   *Chesterfield.*

Things sweet to taste, prove in digestion
sour.   *Shakespeare.*

Dignity.

True dignity is never gained by place,
And never lost when honors are withdrawn.   *Massinger.*

A fit of anger is as fatal to dignity as a dose of arsenic to life.　　*Dr. Holland.*

Diligence.

Who makes quick use of the moment is a genius of prudence.　　*Lavater.*

Dinner.

A good dinner sharpens wit, while it softens the heart.　　*Doran.*

Disappointment.

Out of the same substances one stomach will extract nourishment, another poison; and so the same disappointments in life will chasten and refine one man's spirit, and embitter another's.　　*Wm. Matthews.*

Discipline.

Train up a child in the way he should go; and when he is old he will not depart from it.　　*Prov.* xxii, 6.

Discipline, like the bridle in the hand of a good rider, should exercise its influence without appearing to do so; should be ever active, both as a support and as a restraint, yet seem to lie easily in hand. It must always be ready to check or to pull up, as occasion may require; and only when the horse is a runaway should the action of the curb be perceptible.

Discontent.

Sour discontent that quarrels with our
　　fate
May give fresh smart, but not the old
　　abate;
The uneasy passion's disingenuous wit,
The ill reveals but hides the benefit.
　　　　Sir Richard Blackmore.

What's more miserable than discontent?
　　　　Shakespeare.

Discretion.

Open your purse and your mouth cautiously; and your stock of wealth and reputation shall, at least in repute, be great
　　　　Zimmerman.

There are many shining qualities in the mind of man, but there is none so useful as discretion; it is this, indeed, that gives a value to all the rest, which sets them to work in their proper times and places, and turns them to the advantage of the person who is possessed of them. Without it, learning is pedantry, and wit impertinence; virtue itself looks like weakness; the best parts only qualify a man to be more sprightly in errors, and active to his own principle. *Addison.*

It show'd discretion, the best part of valor. *Beaumont and Fletcher.*

Discretion in speech is more than eloquence. *Bacon.*

Discussion.

Men are never so likely to settle a question rightly as when they discuss it freely. *Macaulay.*

Free and fair discussion will ever be found the firmest friend to truth.
George Campbell.

Disease.

It is not the disease but neglect of the remedy which generally destroys life.
From the Latin.

Dishonesty.

That which is won ill, will never wear well, for there is a curse attends it, which will waste it; and the same corrupt dispositions which incline men to the sinful ways of getting, will incline them to the like sinful ways of spending.
Matthew Henry.

Who purposely cheats his friend, would cheat his God. *Lavater.*

Distance.

'Tis distance lends enchantment to the view,
And robes the mountain in its azure hue.
Campbell.

Divinity.

It is a good divine that follows his own instructions. *Shakespeare.*

There's a divinity that shapes our ends,
Rough-hew them how we will.
Shakespeare.

Dog.

Every dog must have his day.   *Swift.*

Doubt.

When you doubt, abstain.   *Zoroaster.*
To believe with certainty we must be-
gin to doubt.   *Stanislaus.*
Our doubts are traitors
And make us lose the good we oft might
    win
By fearing to attempt.   *Shakespeare.*

Dreams.

Dreams are but interludes that fancy
    makes
When monarch reason sleeps, this mimic
    wakes ;
Compounds a medley of disjointed things.
  *   *   *   *   *
That neither were, nor are not e'er can be.
Sometimes forgotten things, long cast be-
    hind
Rush forward in the brain, and come to
    mind.   *Dryden.*
I ·talk of dreams ;
Which are the children of an idle brain,
Begot of nothing but vain phantasy
Which is as thin of substance as the air ;
And more inconstant than the wind, which
    woos
Even now the frozen bosom of the north,
And, being anger'd, puffs away from
    thence,
Turning his face to the dew dropping
    south.   *Shakespeare.*

Dress.

The person whose clothes are extremely
fine I am too apt to consider as not being
possessed of any superiority of fortune, but
resembling those Indians who are found
to wear all the gold they have in the
world in a bob at the nose.   *Goldsmith.*

79

Drinking.

The first draught a man drinks ought to **be** for thirst, the second for nourishment, **the** third for pleasure, the fourth for madness.

Drunkard.

When he is best, he is little worse than **a** man; and when he is worst he is little **better** than a beast.   *Shakespeare.*

Drunkenness.

Drunkenness is the vice of a good constitution, or of a bad memory! of a constitution so treacherously good, that it **never** bends until it breaks; or of a memory that recollects the pleasures of getting drunk, but forgets the pains of getting sober.   *Colton.*

Duties.

Happy the man, and happy he alone,
He, who can call to-day his own;
He who, secure within, can say
To-morrow do thy worst, for I have lived
        to-day.   *Dryden.*

Be not diverted from your duty by any idle reflections the silly world may make upon you, for their censures are not in your power, and consequently should not be any part of your concern. *Epictetus.*

Stern duty. daughter of the voice of God!
   O, duty! if that name thou love,
Who art a light to guide, a rod
   To check the erring and reprove;
Thou who art victory and law,
When empty terrors overawe,
Give unto me, made lowly wise,
The spirit of self-sacrifice. *Wordsworth.*

Ear.

One ear heard it, and at the other out
        it went.   *Chaucer.*

Early Rising.

The early morning has gold in its mouth.
Franklin.

Early to bed and early to rise,
Makes a man healthy, wealthy and wise.

Few ever lived to a great age, and fewer
still ever became distinguished, who were
not in the habit of early rising.   *Todd.*

Earnestness.

Earnestness alone makes life eternity.
Carlyle.

There is no substitute for thorough going, ardent, and sincere earnestness.
Dickens.

Earth.

The earth, that's nature's mother, is her
tomb.   *Shakespeare.*

The earth is bright,
And I am earthly, so I love it well;
Though heaven is holier, and full of
light
Yet I am frail, and with frail things
would dwell.   *Mrs. Judson.*

And fast by, hanging in a golden chain
This pendant world, in bigness as a star.
Milton.

Ease.

Ease leads to habit, as success to ease.
He lives by rule who lives himself to
please.   *Crabbe.*

Eating.

The chief pleasure (in eating) does not
consist in costly seasoning, or exquisite
flavor, but in yourself.   Do *you* seek
sauce by sweating.   *Horace.*

The turnpike road to people's hearts I find
Lies through their mouths, or I mistake
mankind.   *Dr. Wolcot.*

The difference between a rich man and a
poor man is this—the former eats when he
pleases, and the latter when he can get it.
Sir Walter Raleigh

Eccentricity.

He that will keep a monkey should pay
for the glasses he breaks.   *Selden.*

Echo.

The babbling gossip of the air.
                    Shakespeare.

Economy.

Beware of little expenses; a small leak
will sink a great ship.   *Franklin.*

Economy is of itself a great revenue.
                    Cicero.

Education.

A college education shows a man how
little other people know.   *Haliburton.*

'Tis education forms the common mind.
Just as the twig is bent, the tree's inclin'd.
                    Pope.

All of us who are worth anything, spend
our manhood in unlearning the follies, or
expiating the mistakes of our youth.
                    Shelley.

They who provide much wealth for their
children, but neglect to improve them in
virtue, do like those who feed their horses
high, but never train them to the manage.
                    Socrates.

Effort.

The rider likes best the horse which
needs most breaking in.
                    Edward Garrett.

The general prizes most the fortress
which took the longest siege.
                    Edward Garrett.

The vain beauty cares most for the conquest which employed the whole artillery
of her charms.   *Edward Garrett.*

Egotism.

We often boast that we are never bored,
but yet we are so conceited that we do not
perceive how often we bore others.
                    La Rochefoucauld.

Eloquence.

The clear conception, outrunning the de-
ductions of logic, the high purpose, the
dauntless spirit, speaking on the tongue,

beaming from the eye, informing every feature, and urging the whole man onward, right onward, to his object,—this is eloquence, or rather it is something greater and higher than all eloquence—it is action, noble, sublime, godlike action.   *Webster.*

God gave you that gifted tongue of yours, and set it between your teeth, to make known your true meaning to us, not be rattled like a muffin man's bell.
Carlyle.

Pour the full tide of eloquence along,
Serenely pure, and yet divinely strong.
Pope.

His tongue
Dropp'd manna, and could make the worse appear
The better reason to perplex and dash
Maturest counsels.   *Milton.*

It is but poor eloquence which only shows that the orator can talk.
Sir Joshua Reynolds.

Her tears her only eloquence.   *Rogers.*
Whene'er he speaks, Heaven, how the list'ning throng
Dwell on the melting music of his tongue!
His arguments are emblems of his mien,
Mild but not faint, and forcing, though serene:
And when the power of eloquence he'd try,
Here lightning strikes you, there soft breezes sigh.   *Garth.*

When he spoke, what tender words he us'd!
So softly, that like flakes of feather'd snow,
They melted as they fell.   *Dryden.*

Your words are like the notes of dying swans;
Too sweet to last.   *Dryden.*

True eloquence consists in saying all that should be, not all that could be said.
La Rochefoucauld.

Empire.

Nations and empires flourish and decay,
By turns command, and in their turns obey.   *Ovid.*

Westward the course of empire take its way,

The four first acts already past,
A fifth shall close the drama with the day;
Time's noblest offspring is the last.
Bishop Berkeley.

Emulation.

Keeps mankind sweet by action: without
that
The world would be a filthy settled mud.
Crown.

End.

The end crowns all;
And that old common arbitrator, time,
Will one day end it. *Shakespeare.*

All's well that ends well, still the finis is
the crown. *Shakespeare.*

Endurance.

He conquers who endures. *Persius.*

Enemies.

If you want enemies excel others; if
you want friends let others excel you.
Colton.

The fine and noble way to kill a foe
Is not to kill him; you with kindness may
So change him, that he shall cease to be
so;
Then he's slain. *Aleyn.*

There's not so much danger
In a known foe as a suspected friend.
Nabb,

Ennui.

Give me to drink, Mandragora,
That I may sleep away this gap of time.
Shakespeare.

Enthusiasm.

Nothing is so contagious as enthusiasm; it is the real allegory of the tale of
Orpheus; it moves stones, it charms
brutes. Enthusiasm is the genius of sincerity, and truth accomplishes no victories
without it. *Bulwer.*

Enthusiast.

No wild enthusiast ever yet could rest
'Till half mankind were like himself possess'd. *Cowper.*

Entreaty.

Once more into the breach, dear friends,
once more! *Shakespeare.*

Envy.

The most certain sign of being born with great qualities is to be born without envy.
La Rochefoucauld.

As rust corrupts iron, so envy corrupts man. *Anisthenes.*

Envy is but the smoke of low estate,
Ascending still against the fortunate.
Lord Brooke.

Envy is a weed that grows in all soils and climates, and is no less luxuriant in the country than in the court; is not confined to any rank of men or extent of fortune, but rages in the breasts of all degrees. *Lord Clarendon.*

He who envies another admits his own inferiority. *From the Latin.*

Our envy always lasts longer than the happiness of those we envy.
La Rochefoucauld.

Equality.

In the gates of Eternity, the black hand and the white hand hold each other with an equal clasp. *Mrs. Stowe.*

Equity.

All things whatsoever ye would that men should do unto you, do ye even so to them. *Matt.* vii, 12.

Error.

O, hateful error—Melancholy's child!
Why dost thou show to the apt thoughts of
men
The things that are not? O, Error, soon
conceived!
Thou never coms't unto a happy birth.
But kill'st the mother that engendered
thee. *Shakespeare.*

From the errors of others, a wise man corrects his own. *Syrus.*

I will not quarrel with a slight mistake,
Such as our nature's frailty may excuse.
Roscommon.

A man's errors are what make him amiable. *Goethe.*

85

The best may slip, and the most cautious
    fall;
He's more than mortal that ne'er err'd at
    all.   *Pomfret.*

Great errors seldom originate but with
men of great minds.   *Petrarch.*

Errors like straws upon the surface flow:
He who would search for pearls must dive
    below.   *Dryden.*

Estrangement.

There is not so agonizing a feeling in the
whole catalogue of human suffering, as the
first conviction that the heart of the being
whom we most tenderly love is estranged
from us.   *Bulwer.*

Eternity.

Eternity stands always fronting God;
A stern colossal image with blind eyes,
And grand dim lips, that murmur ever-
    more,
"God, God, God!"   *Mrs. Browning.*

None can comprehend eternity but the
eternal God. Eternity is an ocean, where-
of we shall never see the shore; it is a
deep, where we can find no bottom; a
labyrinth from whence we cannot extricate
ourselves and where we shall ever lose the
door.   *Boston.*

Why shrinks the soul
Back on herself, and startles at destruc-
    tion?
'Tis the divinity that stirs within us;
'Tis heaven itself that points out an here-
    after,
And intimates eternity to man.
Eternity, thou pleasing dreadful thought!
Thro' what variety of untry'd being
Thro' what new scenes and changes must
    we pass?
The wide, the unbounded prospect lies be-
    fore me;
But shadows, clouds, and darkness rest
    upon it.   *Addison.*

Etiquette.

There was a general whisper, toss, and
    wriggle,
But etiquette forbade them all to giggle.
               Byron.

Evening.

The curfew tolls the knell of parting day.
　The lowing herd winds slowly o'er the
　　lea ;
The ploughman homeward plods his weary
　way,
And leaves the world to darkness and to
　me.
Now fades the glimm'ring landscape on
　the sight,
　And all the air a solemn stillness holds,
Save where the beetle wheels his drony
　flight
　And drowsy tinklings lull the distant
　folds.
Save that from yonder ivy-mantled tower,
　The moping owl does to the moon com-
　　plain
Of such as wand'ring near her secret
　bower
　Molest her ancient, solitary reign.
Gray.

The summer day has clos'd—the sun is
　set ;
Well have they done their office, those
　bright hours,
The latest of whose train goes softly out
In the red west.　　　　*Bryant.*

　　Sweet is the hour of rest,
　　　Pleasant the wind's low sigh,
　　And the gleaming of the west,
　　　And the turf whereon we lie.
Mrs. Hemans.

Now stir the fire, and close the shutters
　fast,
Let fall the curtains, wheel the sofa
　round,
And while the bubbling and loud hissing
　urn
Throws up a steamy column, and the cups,
That cheer but not inebriate, wait on each,
So let us welcome peaceful evening in.
Cowper.

　　How still the evening is
As hush'd on purpose to grace harmony !
Shakespeare.

An eve intensely beautiful; an eve
Calm as the slumber of a lovely girl
Dreaming of hope. The rich autumnal
    woods,
With their innumerable shades and color-
    ings,
Are like a silent instrument at rest:
A silent instrument—whereon the wind
Hath long forgot to play.   *Houseman.*

Evidence.

Hear one side, and you will be in the
dark; hear both sides, and all will be
clear.   *Haliburton.*

Evil.

He who will fight the devil with his own
weapons, must not wonder if he finds him
an over-match.   *South.*

The doing evil to avoid an evil cannot
be good.   *Coleridge.*

An evil at its birth, is easily crushed, but
it grows and strengthens by endurance.
    Cicero.

This is the curse of every evil deed
That, propagating still, it brings forth evil.
    Southey.

Timely advis'd, the coming evil shun!
    Prior.

Examinations.

Examinations are formidable even to the
best prepared, for the greatest fool may
ask more than the wisest man can answer.

Example is a living law, whose sway
Men more than all the written laws obey.
    Sedley.

People seldom improve, when they have
no other model but themselves to copy.
    Goldsmith.

Excellence.

Excellence is never granted to man, but
as the reward of labor. It argues, indeed,
no small strength of mind to persevere in
the habits of industry, without the pleasure
of perceiving those advantages which, like
the hands of a clock, whilst they make

hourly approaches to their point, yet proceed so slowly as to escape observation.
Sir Joshua Reynolds.

Excess.

To gild refined gold, to paint the lily,
To throw a perfume on the violet,
To smoothe the ice, or add another hue
Unto the rainbow, or, with taper-light,
To seek the beauteous eye of heaven to
    garnish,
Is wasteful and ridiculous excess.
Shakespeare.

The desire of power in excess caused angels to fall; the desire of knowledge in excess caused man to fall; but in charity is no excess, neither can man or angels come into danger by it. *Bacon.*

Excesses.

The excesses of our youth are drafts upon our old age, payable with interest, about thirty years after date. *Colton.*

Excuse.

An excuse is worse and more terrible than a lie; for an excuse is a lie guarded.
Pope.

And, oftentimes, excusing of a fault,
Doth make a fault the worse by the excuse;
As patches set upon a little breach,
Discredit more in hiding of the fault,
Than did the fault before it was so patch'd.
Shakespeare.

Exertion.

With every exertion, the best of men can do but a moderate amount of good; but it seems in the power of the most contemptible individual to do incalculable mischief. *Washington Irving.*

Expectation.

How slow
This old moon wanes! she lingers my desires,
Like to a stepdame, or a dowager,
Long withering out a young man's revenue. *Shakespeare.*

Experience.

Experience keeps a dear school, but fools will learn in no other, and scarcely in that; for it is true, we may give *advice*, but we cannot give *conduct*. Remember this; they that will not be counseled cannot be helped. If you do not hear reason she will rap you over your knuckles.
Franklin.

I had rather have a fool to make me merry, than experience to make me sad.
Shakespeare.

Ah! the youngest heart has the same waves within it as the oldest; but without the plummet which can measure the depths. *Richter.*

All is but lip wisdom which wants experience. *Sir Philip Sydney.*

Extravagance.

The man who builds and wants wherewith
to pay
Provides a home from which to run away.
Young.

Dreading the climax of all human ills,
The inflammation of his weekly bills.
Byron.

Eye.

An eye like Mars, to threaten and command. *Shakespeare.*

A beautiful eye makes silence eloquent, a kind eye makes contradiction an assent, an enraged eye makes beauty deformed. This little member gives life to every part about us; and I believe the story of Argus implies no more, than that the eye is in every part; that is to say, every other part would be mutilated, were not its force represented more by the eye than even by itself. *Addison.*

The eye sees not itself
But by reflection, by some other things.
Shakespeare.

Eyes with the same blue witchery as those
Of Psyche, which caught Love in his own
    wiles.   *From the Italian.*

       The soft blue eye,
That looks as it had open'd first in heaven,
And caught its brightness from the ser-
    aph's gaze
As flowers are fairest where the sunbeams
    fall.   *Mrs. Hale.*

His eye was blue and calm, as is the sky
In the serenest noon.   *Willis.*

   A gray eye is still and sly;
   A roguish eye is the brown;
   The eye of blue is ever true;
   But in the black eye's sparkling spell
   Mystery and mischief dwell.

   A pair of bright eyes with a dozen
glances suffice to subdue a man; to enslave
him, and inflame; to make him even forget; they dazzle him so, that the past becomes straightway dim to him; and he so
prizes them, that he would give all his
life to possess them. What is the fond love
of dearest friends compared to his treasure? Is memory as strong as expectancy,
fruition as hunger, gratitude as desire?
                 Thackeray.

   Men with grey eyes are generally keen,
energetic, and at first cold; but you may
depend upon their sympathy with real sorrow. Search the ranks of our benevolent
men and you will agree with me.
                Dr. Leask.

   His eyes have all the seeming of a de-
mon's that is dreaming.   *Poe.*
From women's eyes this doctrine I derive;
They sparkle still the right Promethean
    fire;
They are the books, the arts, the acade-
    mies,
That show, contain, and nourish all the
    world,
Else, none at all in aught proves excellent.
             Shakespeare.

Face.
But then her face,
So lovely, yet so arch, so full of mirth,
The overflowings of an innocent heart.

Rogers.

Her face was like an April morn,
  Clad in a wint'ry cloud;
And clay-cold was her lily hand,
  That held her sable shroud.   *Mallet.*

His face was of the doubtful kind;
That wins the eye and not the mind.

Scott.

Facts.
One fact is better than one hundred analogies.

The Right Honorable Gentleman is indebted to his memory for his jests and to his imagination for his facts.   *Sheridan.*

Facts are to the mind the same thing as food to the body. On the due digestion of facts depends the strength and wisdom of the one, just as vigor and health depend on the other. The wisest in council, the ablest in debate, and the most agreeable in the commerce of life, is that man who has assimilated to his understanding the greatest number of facts.   *Burke.*

Fail.
Macbeth.—If we should fail—
Lady M.—We fail?
But screw your courage to the sticking
    place
And we'll not fail.   *Shakespeare.*

In the lexicon of youth, which fate reserves
For a bright manhood, there is no such
    word
As *fail.*   *Bulwer.*

There is not a fiercer hell than failure in a great object.   *Keats.*

Fairies.
Did you ever hear
Of the frolic fairies dear?
They're a blessed little race,
Peeping up in fancy's face,
In the valley, on the hill.
By the fountain and the rill;

Laughing out between the leaves
That the loving summer weaves.
                    Mrs. Osgood.

Oft fairy elves,
Whose midnight revels by a forest side,
Or fountain, some belated peasant sees,
Or dreams he sees, while o'erhead the
        moon
Sits arbitress, and nearer to the earth
Wheels her pale course, they on their mirth
        and dance
Intent, with jocund music charm his ear;
At once with joy and fear his heart re-
        bounds.   *Milton.*

Fairy Land.

Wherever is love and loyalty, great purposes and lofty souls, even though in a
hovel or a mine, there is fairy-land.
                    Kingsley.

Faith.

Faith builds a bridge across the gulf of
        death,
To break the shock blind nature cannot
        shun,
And lands thought smoothly on the fur-
        ther shore.   *Young.*
Nought shall prevail against us, or disturb
Our cheerful faith, that all which we be-
        hold
Is full of blessings.   *Wordsworth.*

Faith is the substance of things hoped
for, the evidence of things not seen.
                    Hebrews xi, 1.

Faith is the soul going out of itself for
all its wants.   *Boston.*

Faith lights us through the dark to
Deity.   *Davenant.*

For modes of faith let graceless zealots
        fight,
His can't be wrong whose life is in the
        right.   *Pope.*

Faith is not reason's labor, but repose.
                    Young.

Works without *faith* are like a fish without water, it wants the element it should
live in. A building without a basis can-

not stand; faith is the foundation, and every good action is as a stone laid.

Feltham.

We should act with as much energy as those who expect everything from themselves; and we should pray with as much earnestness as those who expect everything from God. *Colton.*

Fall.

I've touch'd the highest point of all my
    greatness:
And from that full meridian of my glory
I haste now to my setting. I shall fall,
Like a bright exhalation in the evening
And no man see me more. *Shakespeare.*

Falsehood.

A goodly apple rotten at the heart;
O, what a goodly outside falsehood hath!

Shakespeare.

The seal of truth is on thy gallant form,
For none but cowards lie. *Murphy.*

A lie should be trampled on and extinguished wherever found. I am for fumigating the atmosphere, when I suspect that falsehood, like pestilence, breathes around me. *Carlyle.*

Fame.

Fame is an ill you may with ease obtain,
A sad oppression to be borne with pain;
And when you would the noisy clamour
    drown,
You'll find it hard to lay the burden down.
Cooke.

And what is fame, that flutt'ring noisy
    sound,
But the cold lie of universal vogue?

H. Smith.

In Fame's temple there is always a niche to be found for rich dunces, importunate scoundrels or successful butchers of the human race. *Zimmerman.*

Vain empty words
Of honor, glory, and immortal fame,
Can these recall the spirit from its place,
Or re-inspire the breathless clay with life?
What tho' your fame with all its thousand
    trumpets,

Sound o'er the sepulchres, will that awake
The sleeping dead? *Sewell.*

I courted fame but as a spur to brave
And honest deeds; and who despises
    fame
Will soon renounce the virtues that de-
    serve it. *Mallet.*

If a man do not erect in this age his
own tomb ere he dies, he shall live no
longer in monument than the bell rings,
and the widow weeps. *Shakespeare.*

Fame may be compared to a scold; the
best way to silence her is to let her alone,
and she will at last be out of breath in
blowing her own trumpet. *Fuller.*

Fame is the spur that the clear spirit doth
    raise
(That last infirmity of noble minds)
To scorn delights and live laborious days;
But the fair guerdon when we hope to
    find,
And think to burst out into sudden blaze,
Comes the blind Fury with the abhorr'd
    shears,
And slits the thin-spun life. *Milton.*

Famine.

This famine has a sharp and meagre face;
'Tis death in an undress of skin and bone,
Where age and youth, their landmark
    ta'en away,
Look all one common sorrow. *Dryden.*

Fanatacism.

The Puritans hated bearbaiting not because it gave pain to the bear, but because
it gave pleasure to the spectators.
                            Macaulay.

Fancy.

Tell me where is fancy bred,
Or in the heart, or in the head?
How begot, how nourished?
It is engendered in the eyes,
With gazing fed; and fancy dies
In the cradle where it lies.
                    Shakespeare.

Farewell.

'Twere vain to speak, to weep, to sigh,
  Oh, more than tears of blood can tell
When wrung from guilt's expiring eye,
  Are in the word farewell—farewell.
                              Byron.

Farewell a word that must be, and hath
    been,
A sound which makes us linger;—yet—
    farewell.   *Byron.*

Fashion.

  Fashion, leader of a chatt'ring train,
Whom man for his own hurt permits to
    reign,
Who shifts and changes all things but his
    shape,
And would degrade her vot'ry to an ape,
The fruitful parent of abuse and wrong,
Hold a usurp'd dominion o'er his tongue,
There sits and prompts him to his own dis-
    grace,
Prescribes the theme, the tone, and the
    grimace,
And when accomplish'd in her wayward
    school,
Calls gentleman whom she has made a
    fool.   *Cowper.*

  I see that fashion wears out more apparel than the man.   *Shakespeare.*

  We laugh heartily to see a whole flock
of sheep jump because one did so; might
not one imagine that superior beings do
the same by us, and for exactly the same
reason?   *Greville.*

  Be neither too early in the fashion, nor
too long out of it; nor at any time in the
extremities of it.   *Lavater.*

Fate.

  Heaven from all creatures hides the
book of Fate.   *Pope.*

  What must be, shall be; and that which
is a necessity to him that struggles is little
more than choice to him that is willing.
                              Seneca.

With equal pace, impartial fate,
Knocks at the palace and the cottage gate.
Horace.

Fate steals along with silent tread,
Found oftenest in what least we dread;
Frowns in the storm with angry brow,
But in the sunshine strikes the blow.
Cowper.

Faults.

O wad some pow'r the giftie gie us
To see oursels as others see us!
It wad frae mony a blunder free us,
And foolish notion. *Burns.*

Men have many faults;
Poor women have but two;
There's nothing good they say,
And nothing right they do.
Anon.

Fear.

In politics, what begins in fear usually
ends in folly. *Coleridge.*

In morals, what begins in fear usually
ends in wickedness; in religion, what begins in fear usually ends in fanatacism.
Fear, either as a principle or a motive, is
the beginning of all evil. *Mrs. Jameson.*

Fear is the tax that conscience pays to
guilt. *Sewell.*

The thing in the world I am most afraid
of is fear, and with good reason, that
passion alone in the trouble of it exceeding other accidents. *Montaigne.*

What are fears but voices airy?
Whispering harm where harm is not.
And deluding the unwary
Till the fatal bolt is shot! *Wordsworth.*

Feasting.

It is not the quantity of the meat, but
the cheerfulness of the guests, which
makes the feast. *Lord Clarendon.*

Mingles with the friendly bowl
The feast of reason and the flow of soul.
Pope.

Feeling.

The last, best fruit which comes to perfection, even in the kindliest soul, is, tenderness toward the hard, forbearance toward the unforbearing, warmth of heart toward the cold, philanthropy toward the misanthropic. *Richter.*

A fellow-feeling makes one wondrous kind. *Garrick.*

Fidelity.

Faithful found
Among the faithless, faithful only he;
Among innumerable false, unmov'd,
Unshaked, unseduced, unterrified;
His loyalty he kept, his love, his zeal
Nor number, nor example with him
    wrought
To swerve from truth, or change his constant mind
Though single. *Milton.*

She is as constant as the stars
That never vary, and more chaste than
    they. *Proctor.*

Finery.

All that glisters is not gold,
Gilded tombs do worms enfold.
    Shakespeare.

Finis.

My pen is at the bottom of a page,
Which being finished, here the story ends;
'Tis to be wished it had been sooner done,
But stories somehow lengthen when begun.
    Byron.

Fire.

Behold how great a matter a little fire kindleth. *James iii, 5.*

And where two raging fires meet together,
They do consume the thing that feeds
    their fury. *Shakespeare.*

Fire that's closest kept burns most of all.
    Shakespeare.

Fireside.

The cat's Eden. *Southey.*

Firmness.

I said to Sorrow's awful storm,
  That beat against my breast,
Rage on—thou may'st destroy this form,
  And lay it low at rest;
But still the spirit that now brooks
  Thy tempest raging high,
Undaunted on its fury looks
  With steadfast eye. *Mrs. Stoddard.*

First and Last.

First must give place to last, because
last must have his time to come; but last
gives place to nothing, for there is not
another to succeed. *Bunyan.*

Flatterers.

Of all wild beasts preserve me from a
      tyrant;
Of all tame—a flatterer. *Johnson.*

Hold!

No adulation!—'tis the death of virtue!
Who flatters, is of all mankind the lowest
Save him who courts the flattery.
                              Hannah More.

When flatterers meet the devil goes to
dinner. *Defoe.*

Flattery.

Flattery is a sort of bad money, to
which our vanity gives currency.
                    La Rochefoucauld.

Nothing is so great an instance of ill-
manners as flattery. If you flatter all the
company you please none; if you flatter
only one or two, you affront all the rest.
                              Swift.

Sirs, adulation is a fatal thing—
Rank poison for a subject, or a king.
                              Dr. Wolcot.

Folly.

Sick of herself is folly's character,
As wisdom's is a modest self applause.
                              Young.

None but a fool is always right. *Hare.*

Fool.

For every inch that is not fool is rogue.
                              Dryden.

This fellow is wise enough to play the
  fool;
And, to do that well, craves a kind of wit.
Shakespeare.

The greatest of fools is he who imposes
on himself, and in his greatest concern
thinks certainly he knows that which he
has least studied, and of which he is most
profoundly ignorant.   *Shaftesbury.*

Though thou shouldst bray a fool in a
mortar among wheat with a pestle, yet will
not his foolishness depart from him.
Prov. xxvii, 22.

Fop.

Knows what he knows as if he knew it
  not,
What he remembers, seems to have forgot.
Cowper.

So gentle, yet so brisk, so wondrous sweet,
So fit to prattle at a lady's feet.
Churchill.

The soul of this man is in his clothes.
Shakespeare.

Forbearance.

Whosoever shall smite thee on thy right
cheek, turn to him the other also. And
if any man will sue thee at the law, and
take away thy coat, let him have thy cloak
also.   *Matt.* v, 39.

Use every man after his deserts, and
who shall 'scape whipping.   *Shakespeare.*

Everything has two handles; the one
soft and manageable, the other such as will
not endure to be touched. If then your
brother do you an injury, do not take it
by the hot hard handle, by representing to
yourself all the aggravating circumstances
of the fact; but look rather on the soft
side, and extenuate it as much as is possible, by considering the nearness of the
relation, and the long friendship and familiarity between you—obligations to kindness which a single provocation ought not
to dissolve. And thus you will take the
accident by its manageable handle.
Epictetus.

Forgetfulness.

Of all affliction taught a lover yet
'Tis sure the hardest science to forget.
Pope.

Forgiveness.

'Tis easier for the generous to forgive,
Than for offence to ask it.   *Thomson.*

Forms.

Of what use are forms, seeing at times
they are empty?—Of the same use as bar-
rels, which are at times empty too. *Hare.*

Fortitude.

Brave spirits are a balsam to themselves;
There is a nobleness of mind that heals
Wounds beyond salves.   *Cartwright.*

————Gird your hearts with silent forti-
    tude
Suffering yet hoping all things.
Mrs. Hemans.

Fortune.

To catch dame fortune's golden smile,
    Assiduous wait upon her;
And gather gear by every wile
    That's justified by honor.
Not for to hide it in a hedge,
    Nor for a train attendant;
But for the glorious privilege
    Of being *independent*.   *Burns.*

Fortune brings in some boats that are
not steered.

Fortune is like the market, where, many
times, if you can stay a little, the price
will fall.   *Bacon.*

To be thrown on one's own resources is
to be cast in the very lap of fortune; for
our faculties undergo a development, and
display an energy, of which they were pre-
viously unsusceptible.   *Franklin.*

When fortune means to men most good
She looks upon them with a threat'ning
        eye.   *Shakespeare.*

Fortune is merry,
And in this mood will give us anything.
Shakespeare.

When fortune sends a stormy wind,
Then show a brave and present mind;
And when with too indulgent gales
She swells too much, then furl thy sails.
Creech.

The wheel of fortune turns incessantly round, and who can say within himself, I shall to-day be uppermost.　　*Confucius.*

Free.

Who then is free? The wise man who can command himself.　　*Horace.*

—— Freedom hath a thousand charms to
　　show,
That slaves howe'er contented never know.
Cowper.

Friend.

Give me the avow'd, the erect, the manly
　　foe,
Bold I can meet,—perhaps may turn his
　　blow;
But of all plagues, good heaven, thy wrath
　　can send,
Save, save, oh! save me from the candid
　　friend.　　*Canning.*

Chide a friend in private and praise him in public.　　*Solon.*

To lose a friend is the greatest of all losses.　　*Syrus.*

A friend to everybody is a friend to nobody.　　*Spanish Proverb.*

Friends.

Friend after friend departs;
　　Who hath not lost a friend?
There is no union here of hearts
　　That hath not here its end.
Montgomery.

It is better to decide between our enemies than our friends; for one of our friends will most likely become our enemy; but on the other hand, one of your enemies will probably become your friend.
Bias.

He who hath many friends, hath none.
Aristotle.

Old friends are best. King James used
to call for his old shoes; they were easi-
est to his feet.   *John Selden.*

Purchase not friends with gifts; when
thou ceasest to give, such will cease to
love.   *Fuller.*

A friend in need
Is a friend indeed.

Friendship.

So we grew together,
Like to a double cherry, seeming parted.
But yet a union in partition,
Two lovely berries moulded on one stem:
So, with two seeming bodies, but one
    heart.   *Shakespeare.*

Friendship's the wine of life.   *Young.*
We still have slept together
Rose at an instant, learn'd, play'd, eat to-
    gether;
And wheresoe'er we went, like Juno's
    swans,
Still we went coupled, and inseparable.
                         Shakespeare.

Friendship is no plant of hasty growth;
Tho' planted in esteem's deep fixed soil,
The gradual culture of kind intercourse
Must bring it to perfection.
                    Joanna Baillie.

Great souls by instinct to each other turn,
Demand alliance, and in friendship burn.
                        Addison.

Friendship's the privilege
Of private men; for wretched greatness
    knows
No blessing so substantial.   *Tate.*

—— O friendship! of all things the
Most rare, and therefore most rare, be-
    cause most
Excellent; whose comforts in misery
Are always sweet, whose counsels in
Prosperity are ever fortunate.   *Lilly.*

Friendship is composed of a single soul
inhabiting two bodies.   *Aristotle.*

Friendship is the only thing in the world
concerning the usefulness of which all
mankind are agreed.   *Cicero.*

Frugality.

Frugality may be termed the daughter of prudence, the sister of temperance, and the parent of liberty. He that is extravagant will quickly become poor, and poverty will enforce dependence and invite corruption. *Johnson.*

Fury.

I understand a fury in your words,
But not your words. *Shakespeare.*

Future.

Heaven from all creatures hides the book of fate,
All but the page prescribed, their present fate. *Pope.*

God will not suffer man to have the knowledge of things to come: for if he had prescience of his prosperity he would be careless: and understanding of his adversity he would be senseless. *Augustine.*

There is no hope—the future will but turn
The old sand in the falling glass of time.
R. H. Stoddard.

Trust no future howe'er pleasant!
Let the dead past bury its dead!
Act—act in the living present!
Heart within and God o'erhead!
Longfellow.

The veil which covers the face of futurity is woven by the hand of mercy. *Bulwer.*

Gallantry.

Conscience has no more to do with gallantry than it has with politics. *Sheridan.*

Gallantry consists in saying the most empty things in an agreeable manner.
La Rochefoucauld.

Gambler.

The gamester, if he die a martyr to his profession, is doubly ruined. He adds his soul to every other loss, and by the act of suicide, renounces earth to forfeit heaven. *Colton.*

Look round the wrecks of play behold,
Estates dismember'd, mortgaged, sold;
Their owners now to jail confin'd,
Show equal poverty of mind.   *Gay.*

Bets at the first were fool-traps, where
    the wise
Like spiders lay in ambush for the flies.
                         Dryden.

Some play for gain; to pass time others
    play
For nothing; both play the fool, I say:
Nor time nor coin I'll lose, or idly spend;
Who gets by play, proves loser in the end.
                         Heath.

Gaming is the son of avarice, but the
father of despair.

General.

A gen'ral sets his army in array
In vain, unless he fight and win the day.
                        Denham.

Generosity.

God blesses still the generous thought
    And still the fitting word He speeds,
And truth, at His requiring taught,
    He quickens into deeds.   *Whittier.*

The truly generous is the truly wise;
And he who loves not others, lives unblest.
                        Horace.

Genius.

The three indispensables of genius are
understanding, feeling, and perseverance.
The three things that enrich genius, are
contentment of mind, the cherishing of
good thoughts, and exercising the memory.
                        Southey.

No enemy is so terrible as a man of
genius.   *Disraeli.*

Men of genius are often dull and ·inert
in society, as a blazing meteor when it descends to earth, is only a stone.
                  Longfellow.

Talent, lying in the understanding, is
often inherent; genius, being the action of
reason and imagination, rarely or never.
                  Coleridge.

There is no great genius free from some tincture of madness. *Seneca.*

The greatest genius is never so great as when it is chastised and subdued by the highest reason. *Colton.*

When a true genius appears in the world you may know him by this sign, that the dunces are all in confederacy against him. *Swift.*

Genius and Talent.

Genius is the highest type of reason—talent the highest type of the understanding. *Hickok.*

Gentleman.

A gentleman has ease without familiarity, is respectful without meanness; genteel without affectation, insinuating without seeming art. *Chesterfield.*

His years are young, but his experience old;
His head unmellow'd, but his judgment ripe;
And in a word (for far behind his worth
Come all the praises that I now bestow)
He is complete in feature and in mind,
With all good grace to grace a gentleman.
Shakespeare.

The grand old name of gentleman
Defam'd by every charlatan
And soil'd with all ignoble use.
Tennyson.

Education begins the gentleman, but reading, good company and reflection must finish him. *Locke.*

I am a gentleman,
I'll be sworn thou art!
Thy tongue, thy face, thy limbs, action and spirit,
Do give the five-fold blazon.
Shakespeare.

When Adam dolve and Eve span
Who was then the gentleman? *Pegge.*

Gentleness.

Sweet speaking oft a currish heart reclaims. *Sidney.*

Ghosts.

Glendower.—I can call spirits from the
vasty deep.
Hotspur.—Why so can I, or so can any
man ;
But will they come when you do call for
them ? *Shakespeare.*

Gift.

The manner of giving, shews the character of the giver, more than the gift itself.
Lavater.

Gifts.

Those gifts are ever the most acceptable
which the giver has made precious.
Ovid.

There is no grace in a benefit that sticks
to the fingers. *Seneca.*

Your gift is princely, but it comes too late,
And falls like sunbeams on a blasted blossom. *Suckling.*

Win her with gifts, if she respect not
words ;
Dumb jewels often, in their silent kind,
More quick than words do move a woman's
mind. *Shakespeare.*

And with them, words of so sweet breath
compos'd
As make the things more rich ; their perfume lost,
Take these again ; for to the noble mind
Rich gifts wax poor, when givers prove
unkind. *Shakespeare.*

Never look a gift horse in the mouth.

Glory.

Real glory
Springs from the silent conquest of our-
selves ;
And without that the conqueror is nought,
But the first slave. *Thomson.*

Glory is the fair child of peril. *Smollett.*

Glory, the casual gift of thoughtless
crowds !
Glory, the bribe of avaricious virtue !
Johnson.

Who pants for glory finds a short repose,
A breath revives him, and a breath o'er-
throws. *Pope.*

Our greatest glory consists not in never
falling, but in rising every time we fall.
Goldsmith.

The paths of glory lead but to the grave.
Gray.

Glutton.

Honor's a thing too subtle for his wisdom;
If honor lie in eating, he's right honorable. *Beaumont and Fletcher.*

Gluttony.

Fat paunches have lean pates, and dainty
bits
Make rich the ribs, but bankrupt quite the
wits. *Shakespeare.*

God.

God of my Fathers! holy, just and good!
My God! my Father, my unfailing Hope!
Jehovah! let the incense of thy praise,
Accepted, burn before thy mercy seat,
And let thy presence burn both day and
night. *Pollok.*

A God alone can comprehend a God.
Young.

There is an Eye that never sleeps
  Beneath the wing of night;
There is an Ear that never shuts
  When sink the beams of light.

There is an Arm that never tires
  When human strength gives way;
There is a Love that never fails
  When earthly loves decay.

That Eye is fix'd on seraph throngs:
That Ear is fill'd with angel's songs:
That Arm upholds the worlds on high;
That Love is thron'd beyond the sky.
Heber.

God moves in a mysterious way
  His wonders to perform;
He plants His footsteps in the sea,
  And rides upon the storm. *Cowper.*

All things that are on earth shall wholly
    pass away.
Except the love of God, which shall live
    and last for aye.   *Bryant.*

How calmly may we commit ourselves
to the hands of Him who bears up the
world—of Him who has created, and who
provides for the joy even of insects, as
carefully as if He were their Father!
               Richter.

'Tis hard to find God, but to comprehend
Him, as He is, is labor without end.
               Herrick.

    At whose sight all the stars
    Hide their diminish'd heads.
               Milton.

Gold.

        The picklock,
    That never fails.   *Massinger.*

O cursed lust of gold! when for thy sake
The fool throws up his interest in both
    worlds
First starved in this, then damn'd in that
    to come.   *Blair.*

O, what a world of vile ill-favor'd faults
Look handsome in three hundred pounds a
    year.   *Shakespeare.*

      'Tis gold so pure
It cannot bear the stamp without alloy.
               Dryden.

Good.

That which is good to be done, cannot
be done too soon; and if it is neglected to
be done early, it will frequently happen
that it will not be done at all.
           Bishop Mant.

Hard was their lodging, homely was their
    food
For all their luxury was doing good.
               Garth.

    Good, the more
Communicated, more abundant grows.
               Milton.

Good Breeding.

Virtue itself often offends when coupled
with bad manners.   *Middleton.*

Good breeding shows itself most where, to an ordinary eye, it appears the least.
Addison.

One principal object of good-breeding is to suit our behavior to the three several degrees of men.—our superiors, our equals, and those below us.   *Swift.*

A man's good-breeding is the best security against another's bad manners.
Chesterfield.

The scholar without good-breeding is a pedant, the philosopher a cynic, the soldier a brute, and every man disagreeable.
Chesterfield.

Good-Humor.

Good humor is the health of the soul sadness its poison.   *Stanislaus.*

Good-Nature.

That inexhaustible good nature, which is itself the most precious gift of Heaven, spreading itself like oil over the troubled sea of thought, and keeping the mind smooth and equable in the roughest weather.   *Irving.*

Goodness.

Goodness is beauty in its best estate.
Marlowe.

Kind hearts are more than coronets,
And simple faith than Norman blood.
Tennyson.

He has more goodness in his little finger
Than you have in your whole body.
Swift.

Good-night.

To all, to each, a fair good night,
And pleasing dreams, and slumbers light.
Scott.

Gossip.

For my part I can compare her to nothing but the sun; for, like him, she takes no rest, nor ever sets in one place but to rise in another.   *Dryden.*

Governing.

A man must first govern himself ere he be fit to govern a family, and his family ere he fit to bear the government in the commonwealth.   *Sir Walter Raleigh.*

Government.

It is better for a city to be governed by a good man than by good laws. *Aristotle.*
They that govern most make the least noise. You see, when they row in a barge, they that do drudgery work, slash and puff, and sweat, but he that governs sits quietly at the stern, and is scarce seen to stir.   *Selden.*

For forms of government let fools contest: Whate'er is best administer'd is best.
            Pope.

We are more heavily taxed by our idleness, pride and folly than we are taxed by government.   *Franklin.*

Grace.

Some hae meat that canna eat,
    And some would eat that want it;
But we hae meat, and we can eat,
    Sae let the Lord be thankit. *Burns.*

Gratitude.

        To the generous mind
The heaviest debt is that of gratitude,
When 'tis not in our power to repay it.
            Dr. Thomas Franklin.

The debt immense of endless gratitude.
            Milton.

What is grandeur, what is power?
Heavier toil, superior pain!
What the bright reward we gain?
The grateful mem'ry of the good.
Sweet is the breath of vernal shower,
The bee's collected treasure sweet,
Sweet music's melting fall, but sweeter yet
The still small voice of gratitude. *Gray.*

He who receives a good turn should never forget it; he who does one should never remember it.   *Charron.*

Grave.

The reconciling grave
Swallows distinction first, that made us
foes:
There all lie down in peace together.
Southern.

There the wicked cease from troubling;
and the weary be at rest. There the pris-
oners rest together; they hear not the
voice of the oppressor. The small and
great are there; and the servant is free
from his master. *Job* iii, 17, 18.

A grave, wherever found, preaches a
short and pithy sermon to the soul.
Hawthorne.

Grave-digger.

The houses that he makes, last till
doomsday. *Shakespeare.*

Gravity.

Gravity is a mystery of the body, in-
vented to conceal the defects of the mind.
La Rochefoucauld.

Too much gravity argues a shallow
mind. *Lavater.*

Greatness.

He doth bestride the narrow world,
Like a Colossus; and we petty men
Walk under his huge legs, and peep about
To find ourselves dishonorable graves.
Shakespeare.

In my stars I am above thee, but be not
afraid of greatness; some are born great,
some achieve greatness, and some have
greatness thrust upon them. *Shakespeare.*

Oh! greatness! thou art a flattering dream,
A wat'ry bubble, lighter than the air.
Tracy.

Lives of great men all remind us
    We can make our lives sublime.
And departing leave behind us
    Footsteps on the sands of time;
Footsteps that perhaps another,
    Sailing o'er life's solemn main,
A forlorn and shipwreck'd brother,
    Seeing, shall take heart again.
Longfellow.

What millions died that Cæsar might be
great!   *Campbell.*

The greatest truths are the simplest: so
are the greatest men.

Grief.

And but he's something stain'd
With grief, that's beauty's canker, thou
    might'st call him
A goodly person.   *Shakespeare.*
What a rich feast the canker grief has
    made;
How has it suck'd the roses of thy cheeks!
And drunk the liquid crystal of thy eyes.
                          Sewell.
Oh! grief hath chang'd me since you saw
    me last;
And careful hours, with time's deform'd
    hand,
Have written strange defeatures in my
    face.   *Shakespeare.*
Excess of grief for the deceased is mad-
ness; for it is an injury to the living, and
the dead know it not.   *Xenophon.*
What's gone, and what's past help
    Should be past grief. *Shakespeare*
'Tis impotent to grieve for what is past.
And unavailing to exclaim. *Havard*
            A malady
Preys on my heart, that medicine cannot
    reach
Invisible and cureless.   *Maturin.*
Grief, madam! 'Tis the pensiveness of joy.
Too deep for language—too serene for
    mirth.   *Talfourd.*
Grief knits two hearts in closer bonds
than happiness ever can; and common suf-
ferings are far stronger links than common
joys.   *Lamartine.*
The storm of grief bears hard upon his
    youth,
And bends him like a drooping flower to
    earth.   *Rowe.*
Thine is a grief that wastes the heart,
    Like mildew on a tulip's dyes,—
When hope, deferr'd but to depart,
    Loses its smiles but keeps its sighs.
                          L. E. Landon.

Grudge.

If I can catch him once upon the hip
I will feed fat the ancient grudge I bear
    him.   *Shakespeare.*

Grumbling.

Everyone must see daily, instances of people who complain from a mere habit of complaining.

Guard.

It is better to be always upon your guard, than to suffer once. *Latin Proverb.*

Guest.

A pretty woman is a welcome guest.
        Byron.

    Unbidden guests
Are often welcomest when they are gone.
        Shakespeare.

Guilt.

He swears, but he is sick at heart;
  He laughs, but he turns deadly pale;
His restless eye and sudden start—
  These tell the dreadful tale
That will be told: it needs no words from
    thee
Thou self-sold slave to guilt and misery.
        Dana.

From the body of one guilty deed
A thousand ghostly fears and haunting
    thoughts proceed.   *Wordsworth.*

  So full of artless jealousy is guilt
  It spills itself in fearing to be spilt.
        Shakespeare.

And oh! that pang where more than mad-
    ness lies,
The worm that will not sleep, and never
    dies.   *Byron.*

    God hath yok'd to guilt
Her pale tormentor—misery.   *Bryant.*

Habit.

Habit gives endurance, and fatigue is the best nightcap.   *Kincaid.*

The chain of habit coils itself around the heart like a serpent, to gnaw and stifle it
        Hazlitt.

A new cask will long preserve the tincture of the liquor with which it was first
impregnated.   *Horace.*

Habits.

All habits gather by unseen degrees
As brooks make rivers, rivers run to seas.
                              Dryden.

The diminutive chains of habit are seldom heavy enough to be felt until they are
too strong to be broken.   *Johnson.*

Small habits well pursued, betimes,
May reach the dignity of crimes.
                        Hannah More.

Happiness.

The sweetest bird builds near the ground,
  The loveliest flower springs low;
And we must stoop for happiness
  If we its worth would know.   *Swain.*

That something still   .   .   .
For which we bear to live or dare to die.
                                Pope.

                            How cheap
Is genuine happiness, and yet how dearly
Do we all pay for its base counterfeit!
We fancy wants, which to supply, we dare
Danger and death, enduring the privation
Of all free nature offers in her bounty,
To attain that which. in its full fruition,
Brings but satiety. The poorest man
May taste of nature in her element;
Pure, wholesome, never cloying; while the
      richest,
From the same stores, does but elaborate
A pungent dish of well-concocted poison.
                          J. N. Barker.

I earn what I eat, get what I wear, owe
no man hate, envy no man's happiness,
glad of other men's good, content with my
harm.   *Shakespeare.*

Know then this truth, enough for man to
      know
Virtue alone is happiness below.   *Pope.*

Our happiness in this world depends on
the affections we are enabled to inspire.
                    Duchesse de Praslin.

What nothing earthly gives, or can destroy
The soul's calm sunshine and the heart-
felt joy.   *Pope.*

Perfect happiness, I believe, was never
intended by the Deity to be the lot of one
of His creatures in this world; but that
He has very much put in our power the
nearness of our approaches to it, is what
I have steadfastly believed.   *Jefferson.*

Happiness is in the taste, and not in the
things themselves; we are happy from possessing what we like, not from possessing
what others like.   *La Rochefoucauld.*

Surely happiness is reflective like the
light of heaven; and every countenance,
bright with smiles and glowing with innocent enjoyment, is a mirror, transmitting
to others the rays of a supreme and ever-
shining benevolence. *Washington Irving.*

After long storms and tempests overblown,
The sun at length his joyous face doth
cleare;
So when fortune all her spight hath
showne,
Some blissful houres at last must needs
appeare,
Else should afflicted wights oft-times de-
speare.   *Spenser.*

If solid happiness we prize,
Within our breast this jewel lies,
And they are fools who roam;
The world has nothing to bestow;
From our own selves our joys must flow
And that dear hut—our home.   *Cotton.*

All who joy would win
Must share it—happiness was born a twin.
                                    Byron.

Happiness and Wisdom.

There is this difference between happiness and wisdom; he that thinks himself
the happiest man really is so; but he that
thinks himself the wisest, is generally the
greatest fool.   *Colton.*

Harlot.

She weaves the winding-sheets of souls,
    and lays
Them in the urn of everlasting death.
                                    Pollok.

    'Tis the strumpet's plague
To beguile many, and be beguiled by one.
                              Shaftesbury.

Harvest.

        Glowing scene!
Nature's long holiday! luxuriant—rich
In her proud progeny, she smiling marks
Their graces, now mature, and wonder
        fraught!
Hail! season exquisite!—and hail ye sons
Of rural toil!—ye blooming daughters! ye
Who, in the lap of hardy labor rear'd,
Enjoy the mind unspotted.
                          Mary Robinson.

Haste.

Running together all about,
The servants put each other out,
Till the grave master had decreed,
The more haste, ever the worst speed.
                               Churchill.

Hatred.

    A man should not allow himself to hate
even his enemies, because if you indulge
this passion, on some occasions, it will rise
of itself in others: if you hate your enemies, you will contract such a vicious habit
of mind, as by degrees will break out upon
those who are your friends, or those who
are indifferent to you.   *Plutarch.*

Thou mayst hold a serpent by the tongue,
A chafed lion by the mortal paw,
A fasting tiger safer by the tooth,
Than keep in peace that hand which thou
        dost hold.   *Shakespeare.*

    It is the nature of the human disposition
to hate him whom you have injured.
                                  Tacitus.

Now hatred is by far the longest pleasure;
Men love in haste, but they detest at
        leisure.   *Byron.*

Health.

He who has health has hope, and he who has hope has everything.
Arabian Proverb.

People who are always taking care of their health are like misers, who are hoarding a treasure which they have never spirit enough to enjoy. *Sterne.*

The only way for a rich man to be healthy is, by exercise and abstinence, to live as if he were poor. *Sir W. Temple.*

The common ingredients of health and
    long life are:
Great temp'rance, open air,
Easy labor, little care. *Sir P. Sidney.*

For life is not to live, but to be well.
Martial.

Be sober and temperate, and you will be healthy. *B. Franklin.*

The surest road to health, say what they
    will,
Is never to suppose we shall be ill.
Churchill.

Heart.

Heaven's Sovereign spares all beings but
    himself,
That hideous sight—a naked human heart.
Young.

The honest heart that's free frae a
    Intended fraud or guile,
However fortune kick the ba'
    Has aye some cause to smile. *Burns.*

    A young maiden's heart
Is a rich soil, wherein lie many germs
Hid by the cunning hand of nature there
To put forth blossoms in their fittest sea-
    son ;
And though the love of home first breaks
    the soil,
With its embracing tendrils clasping it,
Other affections, strong and warm will
    grow
While that one fades, as summer's flush of
    bloom
Succeed the gentle budding of the spring.
Mrs. F. Kemble Butler.

The heart aye's the part aye
That makes us right or wrang.
Burns.

I have ease and I have health,
And I have spirits light as air;
And more than wisdom, more than
wealth—
A merry heart that laughs at care.
H. H. Milman.

The human heart is often the victim of
the sensations of the moment; success intoxicates it to presumption, and disap-
pointment dejects and terrifies it. *Volney.*

A recent moralist has affirmed that the
human heart is like a jug. No mortal can
look into its recesses, and you can only
judge of its purity by what comes out of
it. *Anon.*

Heaven.

Heaven is above all yet; there sits a judge
That no king can corrupt. *Shakespeare.*

Heaven's gates are not so highly arch'd
As princes' palaces; they that enter there
Must go upon their knees. *Webster.*

By heaven we understand a state of
happiness infinite in degree, and endless in
duration. *Franklin.*

Eye hath not seen it, my gentle boy;
Ear hath not heard its deep song of joy;
Dreams cannot picture a world so fair;
Sorrow and death may not enter there;
Time doth not breathe on its fadeless
bloom
For beyond the clouds, and beyond the
tomb,
It is there, it is there, my child.
Mrs. Hemans.

A Persian's heaven is easily made,
'Tis but black eyes and lemonade.
Moore.

Heaven and Earth.

Heaven—it is God's throne. The earth
—it is his footstool. *Matthew v, 34.*

Hell.

Hell is truth seen too late. *H. G. Adams.*
Divines and dying men may talk of Hell
But in my heart her several torments
    dwell. *Shakespeare.*
Hell has no limits, nor is circumscribed
In one self place; but where we are is hell
And where hell is, there must we ever be
And to be short, when all the world dis-
    solves,
And every creature shall be purified,
All places shall be hell that are not heaven.
    Marlowe.

Hero.

Whoever, with an earnest soul,
    Strives for some end from this low
        world afar,
Still upward travels though he miss the
    goal,
    And strays—but towards a star. *Bulwer.*

        All may be heroes:—
"The man who rules his spirit," saith the
    voice
Which cannot err,—"is greater than the
    man
Who takes a city." Hence it surely fol-
    lows,
If each man would govern wisely, and
    thus show
Truth, courage, knowledge, power, benevo-
    lence
All, all the princely soul of private virtues,
Then each would be a prince, a hero—
    greater—
He will be a man in likeness of his maker!
    Mrs. Hale.

Heroism.

Heroism—the divine relation which in
all times unites a great man to other men.
    Carlyle.

Highwayman.

Gentlemen of the shade, minions of the
moon. *Shakespeare.*

History.

    Her ample page
Rich with the spoils of time. *Gray.*

Some are to be read, some to be studied, and some may be neglected entirely, not only without detriment, but with advantage. *Bolingbroke.*

Some write a narrative of wars and feats,
Of heroes little known, and call the rant
A history; describe the man of whom
His own coevals took but little note,
And paint his person, character, and
        views,
As they had known him from his mother's
        womb. *Cowper.*

What are most of the histories of the world, but lies? Lies immortalized and consigned over as a perpetual abuse and a flaw upon prosperity. *South.*

Holiness.

Blessed is the memory of those who have kept themselves unspotted *from* the world! Yet more blessed and more dear the memory of those who have kept themselves unspotted in the world.
        Mrs. Jameson.

Home.

Bare walls make a gadding housewife.
        Fielding.

The paternal hearth, that rallying place of the affections. *Washington Irving.*

His warm but simple home where he enjoys
With her who shares his pleasures and his
        heart
Sweet converse. *Cowper.*

Mid pleasures and palaces though we may
        roam,
Be it ever so humble there's no place like
        home. *J. Howard Payne.*

Home is the sacred refuge of our life,
Secured from all approaches but a wife;
If thence we fly, the cause admits no
        doubt,
None but an inmate foe could force us out.
        Dryden.

Honesty.

Honesty coupled to beauty, is to have
honey a sauce to sugar.   *Shakespeare.*

What is becoming is honest, and whatever is honest must always be becoming.
Cicero.

Who is the honest man?
He that doth still and strongly good pur-
sue,
To God, his neighbor, and himself most
true:
Whom neither force nor fawning can
Unpin, or wrench from giving all their
due.   *Herbert.*

Let honesty be as the breath of thy soul,
and never forget to have a penny, when all
thy expenses are enumerated and paid;
then shall thou reach the point of happiness, and independence shall be thy
shield and buckler, thy helmet and crown;
then shall thy soul walk upright, nor stoop
to the silken wretch because he hath
riches, nor pocket an abuse, because the
hand which offers it wears a ring set with
diamonds.   *Franklin.*

Lands mortgag'd may return, and more
esteem'd,
But honesty once pawn'd, is ne'er re-
deem'd.   *Middleton.*

The maxim that "Honesty is the best
policy" is one which, perhaps, no one is
ever habitually guided by in practice. An
honest man is always before it, and a
knave is generally behind it.   *Whately.*

A wit's a feather, and a chief's a rod;
An honest man's the noblest work of God.
Pope.

Heav'n that made me honest, made me
more
Than ever king did when he made a lord.
Rowe.

To be honest, as this world goes,
Is to be one pick'd out of ten thousand.
Shakespeare.

The more honesty a man has, the less he
affects the air of a saint.   *Lavater.*

Honor.

Honor's a good brooch to wear in a man's hat at all times. *Jonson.*

Honor is like that glassy bubble,
That finds philosophers such trouble,
Whose least part crack'd, the whole does
    fly
And wits are crack'd to find out why.
        Butler.

Honor and shame from no condition rise;
Act well your part; there all the honor
    lies. *Pope.*

Honor's a fine imaginary notion.
That draws in raw and unexperienced men
To real mischiefs, while they hunt a
    shadow. *Addison.*

No man of honor, as that word is usually understood, did ever pretend that his honor obliged him to be chaste and temperate, to pay his creditors, to be useful to his country, or to do good to mankind, to endeavor to be wise or learned, to regard his word, his promise, or his oath. *Swift.*
The noblest spur unto the sons of fame,
Is thirst for honor. *John Hall.*

Our own heart, and not other men's opinions forms our true honor. *Coleridge.*

Better to die ten thousand deaths
Than wound my honor. *Addison.*

Woman's honor
Is nice as ermine,—'twill not bear a soil.
    Dryden.

Hope.

It is best to hope only for things possible and probable; he that hopes too much shall deceive himself at last; especially if his industry does not go along with his hopes; for hope without action is a barren undoer. *Feltham.*

Hope
Is such a bait, it covers any hook. *Jonson.*
Come then, oh care! oh grief! oh woe!
  Oh troubles! mighty in your kind,
I have a balm ye ne'er can know,
  A hopeful mind. *F. Vane.*

Auspicious hope! in thy sweet garden grow
Wreaths for each toil, a charm for every
  woe.   *Campbell.*

All, all forsook the friendless guilty mind.
But hope, the charmer, linger'd still behind.   *Campbell.*

Hope deferred maketh the heart sick.
        Prov. xiii, 12.

Hope is the pillar that holds up the
  world.

Hope is the dream of a waking man.
          Pliny.

—Hopes that beckon with delusive gleams,
Till the eye dances in the void of dreams.
         Holmes.

Hope springs eternal in the human breast,
Man never is, but always to be blest.
          Pope.

Hope is a flatterer, but the most upright of parasites; for she frequents the
poor man's hut, as well as the palace of
his superior.   *Shenstone.*

Hope, of all passions, most befriends us
here.   *Young.*

Our greatest good, and what we least can
  spare,
Is hope; the last of all our evils, fear.
        Armstrong.

Hope is like the cork to the net, which
keeps the soul from sinking in despair;
and fear is like the lead to the net, which
keeps it from floating in presumption.
         Watson.

The setting of a great hope is like the
setting of the sun. The brightness of our
life is gone, shadows of the evening fall
around us, and the world seems but a dim
reflection itself—a broader shadow. We
look forward into the coming lonely night;
the soul withdraws itself. Then stars
arise, and the night is wholly.
        Longfellow.

He that loses hope may part with anything.   *Congreve.*

Where no hope is left, is left no fear.
         Milton.

Hope! fortune's cheating lottery
Where for one prize a thousand blanks
    there are.   *Cowley.*

The mighty hopes that make us men.
                Tennyson.

However deceitful hope may be, yet she
carries us on pleasantly to the end of life.
           La Rochefoucauld.

A propensity to hope and joy is real
riches; one to fear and sorrow real poverty.   *Hume.*

True hope is swift and flies with swallow's
    wings;
Kings it makes gods, and meaner crea-
    tures kings.   *Shakespeare.*

Hope is the fawning traitor of the mind,
Which, while it cozens with a color'd
    friendship
Robs us of our best virtue—resolution.
                  Lee.

Hospitality.

Hospitality to the better sort, and charity to the poor; two virtues that are never
exercised so well as when they accompany
each other.   *Atterbury.*

Hours are golden links;—God's tokens
reaching heaven.   *Dickens.*

Catch, then, oh! catch the transient hour,
    Improve each moment as it flies;
Life's a short summer—man a flower;
    He dies—alas! how soon he dies.
                Johnson.

House.

A house is never perfectly furnished for
enjoyment, unless there is a child in it
rising three years old, and a kitten rising
six weeks.   *Southey.*

My precept to all who build is, that the
owner should be an ornament to the house,
and not the house to the owner. *Cicero.*

Nothing lovelier can be found
In woman, than to study household good,
And good works in her husband to pro-
    mote.   *Milton.*

Human Nature.

If we did not take great pains, and were
not at great expense to corrupt our na-

ture, our nature would never corrupt us.
Lord Clarendon
Our humanity were a poor thing were it
not for the divinity which stirs within us.
Bacon.

Humility.

Highest when it stoops
Lowest before the holy throne; throws
down
Its crown abased; forgets itself, admires,
And breathes ador'ing praise.   *Pollok.*
Humility, that low sweet root,
From which all heavenly virtues shoot.
Moore.

The sufficiency of my merit is to know
that my merit is not sufficient.
Augustine.

Humility is a virtue all preach, none
practice, and yet everybody is content to
hear.   The master thinks it good doctrine
for his servant, the laity for the clergy, and
the clergy for the laity.   *Selden.*
Be wise,
Soar not too high to fall, but stoop to rise.
Massinger.
My endeavors
Have ever come too short of my desire
Shakespeare.

Humor.

Let your humor always be good humor
in both senses.   If it comes of a bad humor, it is pretty sure not to belie its pa-
rentage.
Some things are of that nature as to make
One's fancy chuckle while his heart doth
ache.   *Bunyan.*

Hunger.

Famish'd people must be slowly nursed,
And fed by spoonfuls, else they always
burst.   *Byron.*
Hunger is the best seasoning for meat,
and thirst for drink.   *Cicero.*

Hypocrisy.

O serpent heart, hid with a flow'ring face!
Did ever dragon keep so fair a cave?
Shakespeare.

Obey me, features, for one supple moment:
You shall not long be tortured. Here in
   courts
We must not wear the soldier's honest
   face.   *H. Thompson.*

Trust not those cunning waters of his eyes,
For villainy is not without much rheum;
And he long-traded in it, makes it seem
Like rivers of remorse and innocence.
                   Shakespeare.

Thy very looks are lies; eternal falsehood
Smiles in thy lips, and flatters in thine
   eyes.   *Smith.*

The devil can cite Scripture for his pur-
   pose.
An evil soul, producing holy witness,
Is like a villain with a smiling cheek;
A goodly apple rotten at the heart;
Oh, what a goodly outside falsehood hath!
                   Shakespeare.

   Hypocrisy is the homage which vice pays
to virtue.   *La Rochefoucauld.*

Hypocrite.

   The fawning, sneaking, and flattering
hypocrite, that will do, or be anything, for
his own advantage.   *Stillingfleet.*

   Hypocrites do the devil's drudgery in
Christ's livery.   *Matthew Henry.*

Idea.

   An idea, like a ghost, (according to the
common notion of ghost,) must be spoken
to a little before it will explain itself.
                     Dickens.

   He doth nothing but talk of his horse;
and he makes it a great appropriation to
his own good parts, that he can shoe him
himself.   *Shakespeare.*

Idleness.

Absence of occupation is not rest.
A mind quite vacant is a mind distress'd.
                    Cowper.

   Evil thoughts intrude in an unemployed
mind, as naturally as worms are generated
in a stagnant pool.   *From the Latin.*

Sluggish idleness—the nurse of sin.
Spenser.

Idleness travels very slowly, and poverty soon overtakes her. *Hunter.*

Idolatry.

'Tis mad idolatry,
To make the service greater than the god.
Shakespeare.

If.

Your If is the only peace-maker,—
Much virtue in If. *Shakespeare.*

Ignorance.

Where ignorance is bliss
'Tis folly to be wise. *Gray.*
I hardly know so true a mark of a little mind as the servile imitation of another.
Greville.

It is impossible to make people understand their ignorance, for it requires knowledge to perceive it; and, therefore, he that can perceive it hath it not.
Jeremy Taylor.

Ills.

Common and vulgar people ascribe all ill that they feel, to others; people of little wisdom ascribe to themselves; people of much wisdom, to no one. *Epictetus.*

Keep what you've got; the ills that we know are the best. *Plautus.*

Illusion.

Some there be that shadows kiss;
Some have but a shadow's bliss.
Shakespeare.

Imagination.

The beings of the mind are not of clay;
Essentially immortal, they create
And multiply in us a brighter ray
And more beloved existence. *Byron.*

Imitation.

A good imitation is the most perfect originality. *Voltaire.*

Men are so constituted that everybody undertakes what he sees another successful in, whether he has aptitude for it or not.
Goethe.

Immodesty.

Immodest words admit of no defence
For want of decency is want of sense.
Pope.

Immortality.

Immortality o'ersweeps
All pains, all tears, all time, all fears—and peals,
Like the eternal thunders of the deep,
Into my ears this truth—Thou liv'st for ever. *Anon.*

Love, which proclaims thee human bids thee know
A truth more lofty in thy lowliest hour
Than shallow glory taught to human power,
"What's human is immortal!" *Bulwer.*

Impatience.

Impatience dries the blood sooner than age or sorrow. *Creon.*

Implacability.

There's no more mercy in him than there is milk in a male tiger. *Shakespeare.*

Impossible.

Impossible is a word only to be found in the dictionary of fools. *Napoleon I.*

Impressions.

The mind unlearns with difficulty what it has long learned. *Seneca.*

Impudence.

The way to avoid the imputation of impudence is not to be ashamed of what we do, but never to do what we ought to be ashamed of. *Tully.*

What! canst thou say all this and never blush? *Shakespeare.*

Impulse.

Act upon your impulses, but pray that they may be directed by God.
Emerson Tennent.

Since the generality of persons act from impulse much more than from principle, men are neither so good nor so bad as we are apt to think them. *Hare.*

Inaction.

Or doing nothing with a deal of skill.
Cowper.

It is better to have nothing to do, than to be doing nothing. *Attilus.*

Incivility.

A man has no more right to say an uncivil thing, than to act one; no more right to say a rude thing to another, than to knock him down. *Johnson.*

Inconstancy.

The dream on the pillow,
  That flits with the day,
The leaf of the willow
  A breath bears away;
The dust on the blossom,
  The spray of the sea;
Ay,—ask thine own bosom—
  Are emblems of thee.
L. E. Landon.

O heaven! Were man
But constant, he were perfect: that one error
Fills him with faults; make him run through sins:
Inconstancy falls off ere it begins.
Shakespeare.

Independence.

Bow to no patron's insolence; rely
On no frail hopes, in freedom live and die.
Seneca.

Slave to no sect, who takes no private road
But looks through nature up to nature's God. *Pope.*

Industry.

Sloth makes all things difficult, but industry all easy; and he that riseth late, must trot all day, and shall scarce overtake his business at night; while laziness travels so slowly, that poverty soon overtakes him. *Franklin.*

It sweeteneth our enjoyments, and seasoneth our attainments with a delightful relish. *Barrow.*

At the working-man's house hunger looks in, but dares not enter! nor will the bailiff or the constable enter; for industry pays debts, but despair increaseth them.
Franklin.

Inexperience.

He jests at scars who never felt a wound.
Shakespeare.

Infancy.

Heaven lies about us in our infancy.
Wordsworth.

Infant.

Or as the plumage of an angel's wing
   Where every tint of rainbow beauty
   blends. *Mrs. Welby.*

Ere sin could blight, or sorrow fade,
   Death came with friendly care;
The opening bud to heav'n convey'd,
   And bade it blossom there. *Coleridge.*

He smiles and sleeps! sleep on
And smile, thou little young inheritor
Of a world scarce less young; sleep on and
   smile!
Thine are the hours and days when both
   are cheering
And innocent. *Byron.*

Infidelity.

When once infidelity can persuade men that they shall *die like beasts,* they will soon be brought to *live like beasts* also.
South.

Influence.

Not one false man but does unaccountable mischief. *Carlyle.*

As a little silvery circular ripple, set in motion by the falling pebble, expands from its inch of radius to the whole compass of a pool, so there is not a child—not an infant Moses—placed, however softly, in his bulrush ark upon the sea of time, whose existence does not stir a ripple, gyrating outward and on, until it shall have moved across and spanned the whole

131

ocean of God's eternity, stirring even the
river of life, and the fountains at which
the angels drink.   *Elihu Burritt.*

Ingratitude.

I hate ingratitude more in a man,
Than lying, vainness, babbling, drunken-
     ness
Or any taint of vice, whose strong corrup-
     tion
Inhabits our frail blood.   *Shakespeare.*

     Blow, blow thou winter wind,
     Thou art not so unkind
          As man's ingratitude;
     Thy tooth is not so keen,
     Because thou art not seen,
          Although thy breath is rude.
                              Shakespeare.

Injuries.

A man should be careful never to tell
tales of himself to his own disadvantage;
people may be amused, and laugh at the
time, but they will be remembered, and
brought up against him upon some subse-
quent occasion.   *Johnson.*

Innocence.

     O innocence, the sacred amulet,
     'Gainst all the poisons of infirmity,
     Of all misfortunes, injury and death!
                              Chapman.

Against the head which innocence secures,
Insidious malice aims her dart in vain;
Turn'd backwards by the powerful breath
     of heav'n.   *Johnson.*

     There is no courage, but in innocence,
     No constancy, but in an honest cause.
                              Southern.

O that I had my innocence again!
My untouch'd honor! But I wish in vain.
The fleece that has been by the dyer stain'd
Never again its native whiteness gain'd.
                              Waller.

     They that know no evil will suspect
none.   *Ben Jonson.*

     Innocence is always unsuspicious.
                              Haliburton.

Instinct.

In the nice bee what sense so subtly true
From pois'nous herbs extract the healing
   dew?   *Pope.*

By a divine instinct, men's minds distrust
Ensuing danger; as by proof we see
The waters swell before a boisterous storm.
      Shakespeare.

Insult.

Of all the griefs that harass the distress'd,
Sure the most bitter is a scornful jest;
Fate never wounds more deep the generous
   heart,
Than when a blockhead's insult points the
   dart.   *Dr. Johnson.*

Intellect.

The intellect of the wise is like glass; it
admits the light of heaven and reflects it.
      Hare.

Intentions.

A man who is always forgetting his best
intentions, may be said to be a thorough-
fare of good resolutions.   *Mrs. Jameson.*

Intrusiveness.

The great secret of life is never to be in
the way of others.   *Haliburton.*

Irresolution.

I hope when you know the worst you
will at once leap into the river and swim
through handsomely, and not, weather-
beaten by the divers blasts of irresolution,
stand shivering upon the brink. *Suckling.*

Ivy.

As creeping ivy clings to wood or stone
And hides the ruin that it feeds upon.
      Cowper.

Jealousy.

Trifles light as air
Are to the jealous, confirmations strong
As proofs of holy writ.   *Shakespeare.*
    Beware of jealousy.
It is the green-eyed monster which doth
   mock
The meat it feeds on.   *Shakespeare.*

Yet there is one more cursed than them all,
That canker-worm, that monster, jealousy,
Which eats the heart and feeds upon the
    gall,
Turning all love's delight to misery,
Through fear of losing his felicity.
Ah, gods! that ever ye that monster placed
In gentle love, that all his joys defaced!
                                    Spenser.

The venom clamors of a jealous woman
Poison more deadly than a mad dog's
    tooth.   *Shakespeare.*

Jest.

A jest's prosperity lies in the ear
Of him that hears it, never in the tongue
Of him who makes it.   *Shakespeare.*

Jests.

Laughter should dimple the cheek, not
furrow the brow. A jest should be such,
that all shall be able to join in the laugh
which it occasions; but if it bear hard
upon one of the company, like the crack of
a string, it makes a stop in the music.
                                    Feltham.

Jollity.

Give me health and a day, and I will
make ridiculous the pomp of emperors.
                                    Emerson.

Journalism.

A journalist is a grumbler, a censurer, a
giver of advice, a regent of sovereigns, a
tutor of nations. Four hostile newspapers
are more to be feared than a thousand bay-
onets.   *Napoleon I.*

Joy.

Joy descends gently upon us like the
evening dew, and does not patter down
like a hail-storm.   *Richter.*

We show our present joking, giggling race,
True joy consists in gravity and grace.
                                    Garrick.

How much better it is to weep at joy
than joy a weeping.
                                    Shakespeare.

Joys.

Little joys refresh us constantly, like house-bread, and never bring disgust; and great ones, like sugar-bread, briefly, and then bring it. *Richter.*

Judge.

He softens the hard rigor of the laws,
Blunts their keen edge, and grinds their
    harpy claws. *Garth.*

Four things belong to a judge: to hear courteously, to answer wisely, to consider soberly, and to decide impartially.
Socrates.

Judging.

Forbear to judge, for we are sinners all.
Shakespeare.

'Tis better that a man's own works, than that another man's words should praise him. *L'Estrange.*

Every one complains of the badness of his memory, but nobody of his judgment.
La Rochefoucauld.

You think it is a want of judgment that he changes his opinion. Do you think it a proof that your scales are bad because they vibrate with every additional weight that is added to either side? *Edgeworth.*

Justice.

Justice like lightning, ever should appear
To few men's ruin, but to all men's fear.
Swetnam.

1. Do you know me, Mr. Justice?
2. Justice is blind; he knows nobody.
Dryden.

Justice is lame as well as blind among us. *Otway.*

Be just and fear not;
Let all the ends thou aim'st at be thy country's,
Thy God's, and truth's. *Shakespeare.*

Kick.

A kick, that scarce would move a horse
May kill a sound divine. *Cowper.*

Kin.

One touch of nature makes the whole
world kin.   *Shakespeare.*

Kindness.

That best portion of a good man's life
His little nameless, unremembered acts of
    kindness and of love.   *Wordsworth.*

The drying up a single tear has more
Of honest fame, than shedding seas of
    gore.   *Byron.*

King.

                  A crown
Golden in show, is but a wreath of thorns;
Brings danger, troubles, cares, and sleep-
    less nights
To him who wears a regal diadem.
                        Milton.

        Then happy low, lie down!
Uneasy lies the head that wears a crown.
                 Shakespeare.

    A king that would not feel his crown too
heavy for him, must wear it every day;
but if he think it too light, he knoweth not
of what metal it is made.   *Bacon.*

Kiss.

Soft child of love—thou balmy bliss,
Inform me, O delicious kiss!
Why thou so suddenly art gone
Lost in the moment thou art won.
                 Dr. Wolcot.

I came to feel how far above
All fancy, pride, and fickle maidenhood
All earthly pleasure, all imagined good
Was the warm tremble of a devout kiss.
                    Keats.

    My lips pressed themselves involuntarily
to hers—a long, long kiss, burning intense
—concentrating emotion. heart, soul, all
the rays of life's light, into a single focus.
                   Bulwer.

Sweet were his kisses on my balmy lips,
As are the breezes breath'd amidst the
    groves
Of ripening spices on the height of day.
                    Behn.

Kiss the tear from her lip, you'll find the
   rose
The sweeter for the dew.   *Webster.*

Kissing.

Then kiss'd me hard;
As if he pluck'd up kisses by the roots,
That grew upon my lips.   *Shakespeare.*

A pleasing trembling thrills through all
   my blood
Whene'er you touch me with your melting
   hand;
But when you kiss, oh! 'tis not to be spoke.
       Gildon.

Knave.

What a pestilent knave is this same!
       Shakespeare.

A beetle-headed, flat-ear'd knave.
       Shakespeare.

A slippery and subtle knave; a finder out
of occasions; that has an eye can stamp
and counterfeit advantages, though true
advantage never presents itself; a devilish
knave.   *Shakespeare.*

Knowledge.

The first step to knowledge is to know
that we are ignorant.   *Cecil.*

Knowledge is power.   *Bacon.*

The desire of knowledge, like the thirst
of riches, increases ever with the acquisi-
tion of it.   *Sterne.*

The profoundly wise do not declaim
against superficial knowledge in others, as
much as the profoundly ignorant. *Colton.*
He that sips of many arts, drinks of none.
      Fuller.

The shortest and surest way of arriving
at real knowledge is to unlearn the lessons
we have been taught, to remount first
principles, and to take nobody's word
about them.   *Bolingbroke.*

Knowledge of Self.

The most difficult thing in life is to
know yourself.   *Thales.*

Man know thyself! All wisdom centers there. *Young.*

Labor.

It is only by labor that thought can be made healthy, and only by thought that labor can be made happy; and the two cannot be separated with impunity. *Ruskin.*

Where love is there is no labor; and if there be labor, that labor is loved.
Austin.

Numbering sands and drinking oceans dry. *Shakespeare.*

You may as well go about to turn the sun to ice, by fanning in his face with a peacock's feather. *Shakespeare.*

Letting down buckets into empty wells.
And growing old with drawing nothing up. *Cowper.*

Language.

Languages are the pedigrees of nations.
Johnson.

Language is fossil poetry. *Anon.*
When nature's end of language is declined.
And men talk only to conceal the mind.
Young.

Speak the language of the company you are in: speak it purely, and unlarded with any other. *Chesterfield.*

Lark.

Hark! how with lone and fluttering start
The sky-lark soars above,
And with her full, melodious heart,
She pours her strains of love.
Mrs. Welby.

Laughter.

Madness, we fancy, gave an ill-timed birth
To grinning laughter and to frantic mirth.
Prior.

Man is the only creature endowed with the power of laughter; is he not the only one that deserves to be laughted at?
Greville.

How much lies in laughter; the cipher-key wherewith we decipher the whole man! some men wear an everlasting barren simper; in the smile of others lies the cold glitter, as of ice; the fewest are able to laugh what can be called laughing, but only sniff and titter and sniggle from the throat outwards, or at least produce some whiffling, husky cachinnation, as if they were laughing through wool; of none such comes good. The man who cannot laugh is only fit for treasons, stratagems and spoils; but his own whole life is already a treason and a stratagem.   *Carlyle.*

The most utterly lost of all days, is that in which you have not once laughed.
                                          Chamfort.

Law.

The good needs fear no law,
It is his safety, and the bad man's awe.
        Massinger, Middleton and Rowley.

The English laws punish vice; the Chinese laws do more, they reward virtue.
                                          Goldsmith.

To go to law, is for two persons to kindle a fire at their own cost, to warm others, and singe themselves to cinders; and because they cannot agree, to what is truth and equity, they will both agree to unplume themselves, that others may be decorated with their feathers.
                                          Feltham.

Laws.

When the state is most corrupt, then the laws are most multiplied.   *Tacitus.*
Laws can discover sin, but not remove.
                                          Milton.

Lawyers and Physicians.

Commonly, physicians, like beer, are best when they are old, and lawyers, like bread, when they are young and new.
                                          Fuller.

Learning.

A little learning is a dangerous thing!
                                          Pope.

Learning maketh young men temperate, is the comfort of old age, standing for wealth with poverty, and serving as an ornament to riches. *Cicero.*

Lecture.

And every married man is certain
T' attend the lecture called the curtain.
Lloyd.

Leisure.

I am never less at leisure than when at leisure, nor less alone than when I am alone. *Scipio Africanus.*

Lending.

If you lend a person any money, it becomes lost for any purposes of your own. When you ask for it back again, you find a friend made an enemy by your own kindness. If you begin to press still further—either you must part with that which you have intrusted, or else you must lose that friend. *Plautus.*

Letters.

Kind messages that pass from land to
  land,
  Kind letters that betray the heart's deep
    history,
In which we feel the pressure of a hand
  One touch of fire, and all the rest is
    mystery. *Longfellow.*

Letters which are warmly sealed are often but coldly opened. *Richter.*

Liars.

Past all shame—so past all truth.
Shakespeare.

They begin with making falsehood appear like truth, and end with making truth itself appear like falsehood.
Shenstone.

Liberty.

Oh! liberty, thou goddess, heavenly
  bright,
Profuse of bliss, and pregnant with delight! *Addison.*

Liberty! Liberty! how many crimes are committed in thy name. *Madame Roland.*

Oh! give me liberty,
For were ev'n Paradise my prison,
Still I should long to leap the crystal
walls. *Dryden.*

Liberty consists in the power of doing that which is permitted by law. *Cicero.*

Libraries.

Libraries are the shrines where all the relics of the ancient saints, full of true virtue, and that without delusion or imposture, are preserved and reposed.
Bacon.

Lie.

Sin has many tools, but a lie is the handle which fits them all. *Holmes.*

He who tells a lie is not sensible how great a task he undertakes; for he must be forced to invent twenty more to maintain that one. *Pope.*

Life.

Life is but a day at most. *Burns.*

O life! thou art a galling load
Along a rough, a weary road. *Burns.*

My life is but a wind
Which passeth by, and leaves no print behind. *Sandys.*

Life is as tedious as a twice told tale
Vexing the dull ear of a drowsy man.
Shakespeare.

At twenty years of age the will reigns; at thirty, the wit; and at forty, the judgment. *Grattan.*

Our care should not be so much to live long, as to live well. *Seneca.*

Life is real, life is earnest,
And the grave is not its goal;
Dust thou art, to dust returnest,
Was not spoken of the soul.
Longfellow.

Like some fair hum'rists, life is most enjoy'd
When courted least; most worth, when disesteemed. *Young.*

Life's but a walking shadow—a poor
 player,
That struts and frets his hour upon the
 stage,
And then is heard no more. It is a tale
Told by idiot, full of sound and fury
Signifying nothing.   *Shakespeare.*

Nor love thy life, nor hate; but whilst
 thou liv'st
Live well; how long, how short, permit to
 Heaven.   *Milton.*

 That life is long which answers life's
great end.   *Young.*

Live while you live the epicure would
 say
And seize the pleasures of the present
 day;
Live while you live the sacred preacher
 cries,
And give to God each moment as it flies.
Lord in my views let both united be;
I live in pleasure when I live in thee.
     Philip Doddridge.

 To live long, it is necessary to live
slowly.   *Cicero.*

Our life so fast away doth slide
 As doth an hungry eagle through the
  wind;
Or as a ship transported with the tide,
 Which in their passage leave no print
  behind.   *Sir J. Davies.*

The youngest in the morning are not
 sure
That till the night their life they can secure.   *Sir J. Denham.*

 The vanity of human life is like a river,
constantly passing away, and yet constantly coming on.   *Pope.*

Light.

 The first creation of God in the works
of the days was the light of the sense, the
last was the light of the reason; and his
Sabbath work ever since is the illumina-
tion of the spirit.   *Bacon.*

 Ethereal, first of things, quintessence,
pure.   *Milton.*

Is not light grander than fire?   It is
the same element in a state of purity.

> *Carlyle.*

And storied windows richly dight,
Casting a dim religious light.

> *Milton.*

Light-footedness.

Pray you tread softly, that the blind mole
  may not.
Hear a footfall.   *Shakespeare.*

Light-heartedness.

They pass best over the world who trip
over it quickly; for it is but a bog—if we
stop we sink.   *Queen Elizabeth.*

A light heart lives long.   *Shakespeare.*

Lion.

A lion among ladies is a most fearful
thing; for there is not a more fearful
wild-fowl than your lion living.

> *Shakespeare.*

Lips.

Her lips are roses over-washed with dew.

> *Greene.*

Listening.

Were we as eloquent as angels, yet
should we please some men and some
women much more by listening than by
talking.   *Colton.*

Literature.

Literature is the grindstone, to sharpen
the coulters, and to whet their natural
faculties.   *Hammond.*

Living.

The man who will live above his present circumstances is in great danger of
living in a little time much beneath them.

> *Addison.*

From the time we first begin to know,
We live and learn, but not the wiser grow.

> *Pomfret.*

He that spends all his life in sport is
like one who wears nothing but fringes
and eats nothing but sauces.   *Fuller.*

143

Logic.

It was a saying of the ancients, "Truth lies in a well;" and to carry on this metaphor, we may justly say that logic does supply us with steps, whereby we may go down to reach the water.

Dr. I. Watts.

Logician.

He was in logic a great critic,
Profoundly skilled in analytic;
He could distinguish and divide
A hair 'twixt south and southwest side
On either which he would dispute,
Confute, change hands, and still confute.

Butler.

Loquacity.

Learn to hold thy tongue. Five words cost Zacharias forty weeks' silence.

Fuller.

Gratiano speaks an infinite deal of nothing, more than any man in Venice; but his reasons are as two grains of wheat hid in two bushels of chaff; you seek all day ere you find them; and when you have them, they are not worth the search.

Shakespeare.

Love.

Love is the salt of life; a higher taste
It gives to pleasure, and then makes it
    last.   *Buckingham.*

The sweetest joy, the wildest woe is love;
The taint of earth, the odor of the skies
    is in it.   *Bailey.*

Love is not altogether a delirium, yet it has many points in common therewith. I call it rather a discerning of the infinite in the finite—of the ideal made real.

Carlyle.

It is better to have loved and lost,
Than never to have loved at all.

Tennyson.

Love is life's end! an end, but never end-
  ing;
All joys, all sweets, all happiness, award-
  ing;
Love is life's wealth, (ne'er spent, but
  ever spending,)
More rich by giving, taking by discard-
  ing;
Love's life's reward, rewarding in rewarding;
Then from thy wretched heart fond care
  remove;
Ah! shouldst thou live but once love's
  sweets to prove,
Thou wilt not love to live, unless thou
  live to love. *Spenser.*

  Let none think to fly the danger
For soon or late love is his own avenger.
      Byron.

  Love that has nothing but beauty to
keep it in good health is short lived, and
apt to have ague fits. *Erasmus.*

But love is blind, and lovers cannot see
The pretty follies that themselves commit.
     Shakespeare.

Love's a capricious power; I've known it
  hold
  Out through a fever caused by its own
    heat;
But be much puzzled by a cough or cold,
  And find a quinsy very hard to treat.
      Byron.

Love not! love not! the thing you love
  may change,
The rosy lip may cease to smile on you,
The kindly beaming eye grow cold and
  strange,
  The heart still warmly beat, and not for
    you. *Mrs. Norton.*

  The more we love the nearer we are to
hate. *La Rochefoucauld.*

I know a passion still more deeply charm-
  ing
That fever'd youth e'er felt; and that is
  love,
By long experience mellow'd into friendship. *Thomson.*

She never told her love,
But let concealment, like a worm in the
bud
Feed on her damask cheek; she pined in
thought;
And, with a green and yellow melancholy
She sat like patience on a monument,
Smiling at grief.   *Shakespeare.*

Love me little, love me long.   *Marlowe.*

Love will find its way
Through paths where wolves would fear
to prey,
And if it dares enough 'twere hard
If passion met not some reward.   *Byron.*

For the memory of love is sweet,
    Though the love itself were vain
And what I have lost of pleasure,
    Assuage what I find of pain.   *Lyster.*

Love is a god
Strong, free, unabounded, and as some de-
fine
Fears nothing, pitieth none.   *Milton.*

O! love is like the rose,
    And a month it may not see,
Ere it withers where it grows.
                            Bailey.

For oh! so wildly do I love him
That paradise itself were dim
And joyless, if not shared with him.
                            Moore.

Love is not in our choice, but in our
fate.   *Dryden.*

Who loves, raves—'tis youth's phrenzy;
    but the cure
Is bitterer still.   *Byron.*

Love is a passion
Which kindles honor into noble acts.
                            Dryden.

Nuptial love maketh mankind, friendly
love perfecteth it; but wanton love cor-
rupteth and embaseth it.   *Bacon.*

It warms me, it charms me,
    To mention but her name;
It heats me, it beats me,
    And set me a' on flame.   *Burns.*

All the passions make us commit faults;
love makes us commit the most ridiculous
ones.   *La Rochefoucauld.*

Men have died from time to time, and
worms have eaten them, but not for love.
                         Shakespeare.

To write a good love-letter you ought to
begin without knowing what you mean to
say, and to finish without knowing what
you have written.   *Rousseau.*

Love's like the measles—all the worse
when it comes late in life.   *Jerrold.*

Love is merely madness; and I tell you,
deserves as well a dark house and a whip,
as madmen do; and the reason why they
are not so punished and cured, is that the
lunacy is so ordinary, that the whippers
are in love too.   *Shakespeare.*

If you cannot inspire a woman with love
of you, fill her above the brim with love
of herself;—all that runs over will be
yours.   *Colton.*

A mother's love!
If there be one thing pure,
Where all beside is sullied,
That can endure,
When all else passes away;
If there be aught
Surpassing human deed or word, **or**
         thought,
         It is a mother's love.
              Marchioness de Spadara.

What *is* a mother's love?
A noble, pure, and tender flame
Enkindled from above.
                    James Montgomery.

Love moderately; long love doth so;
Too swift arrives as tardy as too slow.
                         Shakespeare.

When love's well-timed, 'tis not a fault to
         love;
The strong, the brave, the virtuous, and
         the wise,
Sink in the soft captivity together.
                         Addison.

         Love did his reason blind,
And love's the noblest frailty of the mind.
                         Dryden.

Love is a pearl of purest hue,
  But stormy waves are round it;
And dearly may a woman rue,
  The hour that first she found it.
                          L. E. Landon.

When poverty comes in at the door, love
flies out at the window.

No cord or cable can draw so forcible,
or bind so fast, as love can do with only
a single thread.   *Burton.*

Man while he loves, is never quite de-
      praved,
And woman's triumph is a lover saved.
                                  Lamb.

Is there no way to bring home a wandering sheep, but by worrying him to
death?   *Fuller.*

To love and to be wise is scarcely
granted to the highest.   *Laberius.*

Love, the sole disease thou canst not
cure.   *Pope.*

Who ever loved that loved not at first
sight?   *Marlowe.*

Love is strong as death. Many waters
cannot quench love, neither can the floods
drown it; if a man would give all the
substance of his house for love, it would
utterly be contemned.
                  Solomon's Song viii, 6, 7.

To her love was like the air of heaven,
—invisible, intangible; it yet encircled
her soul, and she knew it; for in it was
her life.   *Miss M'Intosh.*

All thoughts, all passions, all delights,
Whatever stirs this mortal frame,
All are but ministers of love,
And feed his sacred frame.   *Coleridge.*

The first symptom of love in a young
man is timidity, in a girl it is boldness.
The two sexes have a tendency to approach, and each assumes the qualities
of the other.   *Victor Hugo.*

That you may be loved be amiable.
                                    Ovid.

All love at first, like gen'rous wine,
Ferments and frets until 'tis fine,
But when 'tis settled on the lee,
And from the impurer matter free,
Becomes the richer still the older,
And proves the pleasanter the colder.
Butler.

The proverb holds, that to be wise and
love,
Is hardly granted to the gods above.
Dryden.

Alas! the love of women! it is known
To be a lovely and a fearful thing;
For all of theirs upon that die is thrown,
And if 'tis lost, life has no more to bring
To them but mockeries of the past alone.
Byron.

The wound's invisible
That love's keen arrows make.
Shakespeare.

Love and Friendship.

Friendship often ends in love; but love
in friendship never. *Colton.*

Lover.

If I freely may discover
What should please me in my lover,
I would have her fair and witty,
Savouring more of court than city;
A little proud, but full of pity;
Light and humorous in her toying,
Oft building hopes, and soon destroying,
Long, but sweet in the enjoying;
Neither too easy nor too hard;
All extremes I would have bar'd.
Ben. Jonson.

A lover's like a hunter—if the game be
got with too much ease he cares not for't.
Mead.

In lover's quarrels, the party that loves
most is always most willing to acknowl-
edge the greater fault. *Scott.*

Doubt thou the stars are fire!
Doubt that the sun doth move;
Doubt truth to be a liar;
But never doubt I love.
Shakespeare.

A reserved lover, it is said, always makes a suspicious husband.   *Goldsmith.*

Yet, if thou swear'st,
Thou may'st prove false; at lover's vows,
They say, Jove laughs.   *Shakespeare.*

O, men's vows are women's traitors.
Shakespeare.

Lust.

Capricious, wanton, bold, and brutal lust
Is meanly selfish; when resisted, cruel;
And, like the blast of pestilential winds,
Taints the sweet bloom of nature's fairest
    forms.   *Milton.*

Luxury.

War destroys men, but luxury mankind
At once corrupts the body and the mind.
Crown.

Lying.

And he that does one fault at first,
And lies to hide it, makes it two.
Isaac Watts.

He who has not a good memory, should never take upon him the trade of lying.
Montaigne.

Madness.

How pregnant, sometimes, his replies are!
A happiness that often madness hits on,
Which sanity and reason could not be
So prosp'rously deliver'd of.
Shakespeare.

I am not mad; I would to heaven I
    were!
For then, 'tis like I should forget my-
    self;
O, if I could, what grief should I forget!
Shakespeare.

There is a pleasure in being mad,
Which none but madmen know.
Dryden.

Great wits are sure to madness near al-
    lied,
And thin partitions do their bounds di-
    vide.
Dryden,

Maiden.

Maidens, like moths, are ever caught by
    glare,
And mammon wins his way where seraphs
    might despair.   *Byron.*

A child no more! a maiden now—
A graceful maiden, with a gentle brow;
A cheek tinged lightly and a dove-like
    eye;
And all hearts bless her as she passes by.
                    Mary Howitt.

Main Chance.

As the ancients say wisely
Have a care o' th' main chance;
And look before you ere you leap;
For as you sow, y' are like to reap.
                    Butler.

Man.

God made him, and therefore let him
pass for a man.   *Shakespeare.*

Like a man made after supper of a
cheese-paring; when he was naked, he
was, for all the world, like a forked rad-
ish, with a head fantastically carved upon
it with a knife.   *Shakespeare.*

Know thou this:—that men
Are as the time is.   *Shakespeare.*

What a piece of work is man! How
noble in reason; how infinite in faculties;
in form and moving, how express and
admirable! In action, how like an angel;
in apprehension, how like a god; the
beauty of the world—the paragon of animals! And yet to me what is this quintessence of dust?   *Shakespeare.*

Every man is a volume, if you know
how to read him.   *Channing.*

Men are but children of a larger
growth.   *Dryden.*

He is the whole encyclopedia of facts.
The creation of a thousands forests is in
one acorn; and Egypt, Greece, Rome,
Gaul, Britain, America, lie folded already
in the first man.   *Emerson.*

151

Men are machines, with all their boasted
    freedom,
Their movements turn upon some favor-
    ite passion;
Let art but find the foible out,
We touch the spring and wind them at
    our pleasure.   *Brooke.*

The way to conquer men is by their pas-
    sions;
Catch but the ruling foibles of their
    hearts,
And all their boasted virtues shrink be-
    fore you.   *Tolson.*

A man he seems of cheerful yesterdays
and confident to-morrows.
        Wordsworth.

Men are born with *two* eyes, but with
one tongue, in order that they should see
twice as much as they say.   *Colton.*

The mind of man is vastly like a hive;
His thoughts are busy ever—all alive;
    But here the simile will go no further;
For bees are making honey, one and all;
Man's thoughts are busy in producing
    gall,
    Committing, as it were, self-murther.
        Dr. Wolcot.

O man! while in thy early years,
    How prodigal of times,
Misspending all thy precious hours,
    Thy glorious youthful prime!
Alternate follies take the sway;
    Licentious passions burn;
Which tenfold force give nature's law,
    That man was made to mourn.
        Burns.

Beware the fury of a patient man.
        Dryden.

Know then thyself; presume not God to
    scan;
The proper study of mankind is man.
        Pope.

Manners.

Of manners gentle, of affections mild;
In wit a man, simplicity a child. *Pope.*

Evil habits soil a fine dress more than mud; good manners, by their deeds, easily set off a lowly garb. *Plautus.*

Nothing so much prevents our being natural as the desire of appearing so.
La Rochefoucauld.

Those that are good manners at the court are as ridiculous in the country, as the behavior of the country is most mockable at the court. *Shakespeare.*

Marriage.

Hail, wedded love, mysterious law, true source
Of human offspring, sole propriety
In paradise of all things common else!
Milton.

The best time for marriage will be towards thirty, for as the younger times are unfit, either to choose or to govern a wife and family, so, if thou stay long, thou shalt hardly see the education of thy children, who, being left to strangers, are in effect lost; and better were it to be unborn than ill-bred; for thereby thy posterity shall either perish or remain a shame to thy name. *Sir Walter Raleigh.*

Domestic happiness, thou only bliss
Of paradise that has survived the fall.
Cowper.

Marriage is a feast where the grace is sometimes better than the feast. *Colton.*

The moment a woman marries, some terrible revolution happens in her system; all her good qualities vanish, presto, like eggs out of a conjuror's box. 'Tis true that they appear on the other side of the box, but for the husband they are gone forever. *Bulwer.*

First get an absolute conquest over thyself, and then thou wilt easily govern thy wife. *Fuller.*

Masters and Servants.

If thou art a master, be sometimes blind; if a servant, sometimes deaf.
Fuller.

Maxims.

Maxims are the condensed good sense of nations.   *Sir J. Mackintosh.*

Medicines.

Joy. temperance, and repose,
Slam the door on the doctor s nose.
                    Longfellow.

Mediocrity.

Persevering mediocrity is much more respectable, and unspeakably more useful than talented inconstancy.
          Dr. James Hamilton.

Meditation.

Though reading and conversation may furnish us with many ideas of men and things, yet it is our own meditation must form our judgment.   *Dr. I. Watts.*

Melancholy.

Melancholy is the nurse of frenzy.
          Shakespeare.

Go, you may call it madness, folly,—
  You shall not chase my gloom away;
There's such a charm in melancholy,
  I would not, if I could, be gay!
                    Rogers.

        Melancholy
Sits on me, as a cloud along the sky,
Which will not let the sunbeams through.
    nor yet
Descend in rain, and end, but spreads it-
    self
Twixt heaven and earth, like envy be-
    tween man
And man—an everlasting mist.   *Byron.*

Memory.

Lull'd in the countless chambers of the
    brain,
Our thoughts are link'd by many a hidden
    chain;
Awake but one, and lo, what myriads rise!
Each stamps its image as the other flies.
                    Pope.

Tears, idle tears, I know not what they
    mean,
Tears from the depth of some divine de-
    spair,
Rise in the heart and gather in the eyes,
In looking on the happy autumn fields
And thinking of the days that are no
    more.   *Tennyson.*

A strong memory is generally coupled
with an infirm judgment.   *Montaigne.*

Men.

Men are the sport of circumstances,
when the circumstances seem the sport of
men.   *Byron.*

There are but three classes of men: *the
retrograde, the stationary* and *the progres-
sive.*   *Lavater.*

It is far easier to know men than to
know man.   *La Rochefoucauld.*

Never have anything to do with an unlucky place, or an unlucky man. I have
seen many clever men, very clever men,
who had not shoes to their feet. I never
act with them. Their advice sounds very
well, but they cannot get on themselves;
and if they cannot do good to themselves,
how can they do good to me?
                Rothschild.

Men, Great.

Lives of great men all remind us,
    We can make our lives sublime,
And departing, leave behind us
    Footprints in the sands of time.

Footprints, that perhaps another,
    Sailing o'er life's solemn main,
A forlorn and shipwreck'd brother,
    Seeing, shall take heart again.
                Longfellow.

Mercy.

The quality of mercy is not strain'd:
It droppeth, as the gentle rain from
    heaven
Upon the place beneath; it is twice
    bless'd,
It blesseth him that gives, and him that
    takes:

'Tis mightiest in the mightiest: it becomes
The throned monarch better than his crown:
His sceptre shows the force of temporal power,
The attribute to awe and majesty,
Wherein doth sit the dread and fear of kings;
But mercy is above this scepter'd sway,
It is an attribute to God himself;
And earthly power doth then show likest God's,
When mercy seasons justice.
                 Consider this,—
That, in the course of justice, none of us
Should see salvation: we do pray for mercy;
And that same prayer doth teach us all to render
The deeds of mercy.   *Shakespeare.*

Merit.

Modesty is to merit as shades to figures in a picture; giving it strength and beauty.   *La Bruyère.*

Good actions crown themselves with lasting bays
Who deserves well, needs not another's praise.   *Heath.*

Metaphysics.

He knew what's what, and that's as high
As metaphysics wit can fly.   *Meta.*

Midnight.

Midnight,—strange mystic hour,—when the veil between the frail present and the eternal future grows thin.   *Mrs. Stowe.*

Mind.

My mind to me an empire is.
      Southwell.

In my mind's eye, Horatio.
      Shakespeare.

A mind content both crown and kingdom is.   *Greene.*

Cultivation to the mind is as necessary
as food to the body.   *Cicero.*

Canst thou not minister to a mind dis-
    eased;
Pluck from the memory a rooted sorrow;
Raze out the written troubles of the brain;
And, with some sweet oblivious antidote,
Cleanse the foul bosom of that perilous
    stuff
Which weighs upon the heart?
                    Shakespeare.

'Tis the mind that makes the body rich.
                    Shakespeare.

It is the mind that maketh good or ill,
That maketh wretch or happy, rich or
    poor.   *Spenser.*

A narrow mind begets obstinacy, and
we do not easily believe what we cannot
see.   *Dryden.*

The mind ought sometimes to be diverted, that it may return the better to
thinking.   *Phoedrus.*

A weak mind is like a microscope, which
magnifies trifling things, but cannot receive great ones.   *Chesterfield.*

        Ah! noblest minds
Sink soonest into ruin; like a tree,
That with the weight of its own golden
    fruitage
Is bent down to the dust.   *H. Neele.*

Minister.

Of right and wrong he taught
Truths as refined as ever Athens heard;
And (strange to tell!) he practised what
    he preach'd.   *Armstrong.*

The life of a pious minister is visible
rhetoric.   *Hooker.*

It would be well, if some who have
taken upon themselves the ministry of the
Gospel, that they would first preach to
themselves, then afterwards to others.
                  Cardinal Pole.

Mirth.

O spirits gay, and kindly heart!
Precious the blessings ye impart!
            Joanna Baillie.

From the crown of his head to the sole
of his foot he is all mirth; he has twice
or thrice cut Cupid's bowstring, and the
little hangman dare not shoot at him:
he hath a heart as sound as a bell, and
his tongue is the clapper; for what his
heart thinks his tongue speaks.

Shakespeare.

Jest and youthful jollity,
Quips, and cranks, and wanton wiles,
Nods and becks, and wreathed smiles.

Milton.

Care to our coffin adds a nail, no doubt;
And ev'ry grin so merry, draws one out.

Dr. Wolcot.

Misanthrope.

I am *misanthropos,* and hate mankind.
For thy part, I do wish thou wert a dog,
That I might love thee something.

Shakespeare.

As prone to mischief, as able to perform
it. *Shakespeare.*

Miser.

Some o'er-enamour'd of their bags, run
mad;
Groan under gold, yet weep for want of
bread. *Young.*

I can compare our rich misers to nothing so fitly as to a whale; that plays and
tumbles, driving the poor fry before him,
and at last devours them all at a mouth-
ful. *Shakespeare.*

Misery.

This iron world
Brings down the stoutest hearts to lowest
state:
For misery doth bravest minds abate.

Spenser.

Misfortune.

Misfortune, like a creditor severe,
But rises in demand for her delay;
She makes a scourge of past prosperity
To sting thee more and double thy dis-
tress. *Young.*

Mistrust.

I hold it cowardice,
To rest mistrustful, where a noble heart
Hath pawn'd an open hand in sign of love.
Shakespeare.

It is more disgraceful to distrust than
to be deceived by our friends.
La Rochefoucauld.

The world is an old woman, that mistakes any gilt farthing for a gold coin;
whereby being often cheated, she will
henceforth trust nothing but the common
copper. *Carlyle.*

Modesty.

The crimson glow of modesty o'erspread
Her cheek, and gave new lustre to her
charms. *Dr. Thomas Franklin.*
The violet droops its soft and bashful
brow,
But from its heart sweet incense fills
the air ;—
So rich within—so pure without—art
thou,
With modest mien and soul of virtue
rare. *Mrs. Osgood.*
They oft-times take more pains
Who look for pins, than those who find
out stars. *John Fountain.*

Moments.

Think nought a trifle, though it small appear ;
Small sands the mountain, moments make
the year,
And trifles life. *Young.*

Money.

If you make money your god, it will
plague you like the devil. *Fielding.*
Mammon has enriched his thousands,
and has damned his ten thousands.
South.

The love of money is the root of all
evil ; which while some coveted after they
have erred from the faith, and pierced
themselves through with many sorrows.
I Tim. vi, 10.

For they say, if money go before, all ways do lie open. *Shakespeare.*

Money is a good servant, but a dangerous master. *Bonhours.*

Put not your trust in money, but put your money in trust. *Holmes.*

He that wants money, means and content, is without three good friends.

Shakespeare.

Moon.

The cold chaste Moon, the Queen of
    Heaven's bright isles,
Who makes all beautiful on which she
    smiles!
That wandering shrine of soft, yet icy
    flame,
Which ever is transform'd yet still the
    same,
And warms, but not illumines. *Shelley.*

          The queen of night
Shines fair with all her virgin stars about
    her. *Otway.*

Now through the passing clouds she seems
    to stoop,
Now up the pure cerulean rides sublime.
Wide the pale deluge floats, and stream-
    ing mild
O'er the sky'd mountain to the shadowy
    vale,
While rocks and floods reflect the quiver-
    ing gleam,
The whole air whitens with a boundless
    tide
Of silver radiance, trembling round the
    world. *Thomson.*

Moral Law.

The moral law is written on the tablets of eternity. For every false word or unrighteous deed, for cruelty and oppression, for lust or vanity, the price has to be paid at last. *J. A. Froude.*

Morning.

But, look, the morn in russet mantle clad
Walks o'er the dew of yon high eastern
    hill. *Shakespeare.*

Now from night's womb the glorious **day**
    breaks forth,
And seems to kindle from the setting
    stars.   *Lee.*

Morn, in the white wake of the morning
    star,
Came furrowing all the orient into gold.
        Tennyson.

Now morn her rosy steps in th' eastern
    clime
Advancing, sow'd the earth with orient
    pearl.   *Milton.*

Mother.

She was my friend—I had but her—no
    more,
No other upon earth—and as for heaven,
I am as they that seek a sign, to whom
No sign is given. My mother! Oh, my
    mother!   *Taylor.*

    A mother is a mother still,
    The holiest thing alive. *Coleridge.*

Mourning.

None acted mourning forced to show,
Or squeeze his eyes to make the torrent
    flow.   *Dryden.*

Excess of grief for the deceased is madness; for it is an injury to the living, and
the dead know it not.   *Xenophon.*

Murmuring.

Murmur at nothing: if our ills are re-
parable, it is ungrateful; if remediless, it
is vain.   *Shakespeare.*

Music.

The man that hath no music in himself,
Nor is not moved with concord of sweet
    sounds,
Is fit for treasons, stratagems and spoils;
The motions of his spirit are dull **as**
    night,
And his affections dark as Erebus;
Let no such man be trusted.
        Shakesbeare.

Music hath charms to soothe a savage
breast,
To soften rocks, or bend a knotted oak.
I've read that things inanimate have
moved,
And as with living souls have been in-
form'd
By magic numbers and persuasive sound.
Congreve.

There's music in the sighing of a reed;
There's music in the gushing of a rill;
There's music in all things, if men had
ears
Their earth is but an echo of the spheres.
Byron.

Name.

He left a name, at which the world grew
pale,
To point a moral, or adorn a tale.
Johnson.

Nature.

The sea is like a silvery lake,
And o'er its calm the vessel glides
Gently as if it fear'd to wake
The slumbers of the silent tides.
Moore.

Man's rich with little, were his judgment
true;
Nature is frugal, and her wants are few;
These few wants, answer'd bring sincere
delights;
But fools create themselves new appetites.
Young.

All things are artificial, for
Nature is the art of God.
Sir Thos. Browne.

Surely there is something in the unruf-
fled calm of nature that overawes our little anxieties and doubts: the sight of the
deep-blue sky, and the clustering stars
above, seems to impart a quiet to the
mind. *Edwards.*

To him who in the love of nature holds
Communion with her visible forms, she
speaks
A various language. *Bryant.*

Nature the vicar of the Almighty Lord.
Chaucer.

One impulse from a vernal wood
  May teach you more of man,
Of moral evil and of good,
  Than all the sages can.
Wordsworth.

Nature and Art.

Nature is mighty. Art is mighty. Artifice is weak. For nature is the work of a mightier power than man. Art is the work of man under the guidance and inspiration of a mightier power. Artifice is the work of mere man in the imbecility of his mimic understanding. *Anon.*

Nature is the chart of God, mapping out all His attributes: art is the shadow of His wisdom, and copieth His resources.
Tupper.

Necessity.

The tyrant's plea. *Milton.*

When fear admits no hope of safety,
Necessity makes dastards valiant men.
Herrick.

Necessity is the mother of invention.

Neck.

A lover forsaken
  A new love may get;
But a neck that's once broken
  Can never be set. *Walsh.*

Negligence.

A little fire is quickly trodden out;
Which being suffer'd, rivers cannot
  quench. *Shakespeare.*

Omittance is no quittance.
Shakespeare.

Negotiation.

It is better to sound a person with whom one deals afar off, than to fall upon the point at first. *Bacon.*

Nervousness.

He experienced that nervous agitation to which brave men as well as cowards are subject; with this difference, that the

163

one sinks under it, like the vine under the
hailstorm, and the other collects his en-
ergies to shake it off, as the cedar of Leb-
anon is said to elevate its boughs to disperse the snow which accumulates upon
them.   *Sir Walter Scott.*

New.

Nothing is new; we walk where others
    went;
There's no vice now but has its precedent.
                             Herrick.

News.

For evil news rides post, while good
news baits.   *Milton.*

Newspapers.

An abstract and brief chronicle of the
times.

Every editor of newspapers pays tribute
to the Devil.   *La Fontaine.*

Nickname.

A nickname is the heaviest stone the
devil can throw at a man.   *Anon.*

A good name will wear out; a bad one
may be turned; a nickname lasts forever.   *Zimmerman.*

Night.

Night whose sable hand
Hangs on the purple skirts of flying day.
                             Dyer.

Why does the evening, does the night,
put warmer love in our hearts? Is it the
nightly pressure of helplessness? or is it
the exalting separation from the turmoils
of life, that veiling of the world in which
for the soul nothing there remains but
souls? Is it therefore that the letters in
which the loved name stands written in
our spirit appears like phosphorous writing by night, *in fire,* while by day, in their
cloudy traces, they but smoke? *Richter.*

How like a widow in her weeds, the night,
Amid her glimmering tapers, silent sits!
How sorrowful, how desolate, she weeps
Perpetual dews, and saddens nature's
    scene.   *Young.*

In her starry shade
Of dim and solitary loveliness,
I learn the language of another world.
Byron.

Nobility.

Better not be at all,
Than not be noble. *Tennyson.*

Would'st thou clearly learn what true
nobility is? inquire of noble-minded
women. *German Saying.*

He is noble only who in word, thought
and deed, proves himself a man. *Anon.*

Nonsense.

A little nonsense now and then,
Is relish'd by the best of men. *Anon.*

Nonsense and noise will oft prevail,
When honor and affection fail. *Lloyd.*

Novels.

Writers of novels and romances in general bring a double loss on their readers,
they rob them both of their time and
money; representing men, manners, and
things, that never have been, nor are likely to be; either confounding or perverting
history or truth, inflating the mind, or
committing violence upon the understanding. *Lady Montague.*

Novelty.

Of all the passions that possess mankind,
The love of novelty rules most the mind;
In search of this, from realm to realm we
roam;
Our fleets come fraught with ev'ry folly
home. *Foote.*

Now.

Now! it is gone.—Our brief hours travel
post,
Each with its thought or deed, its why or
how;
But know, each parting hour gives up a
ghost
To dwell within thee—an eternal now!
Coleridge.

Oak.

The monarch oak, the patriarch of the
    trees,
Shoots rising up, and spreads by slow de-
    grees:
Three centuries he grows, and three he
    stays
Supreme in state; and in three more de-
    cays.   *Dryden.*

Oaths.

An oath is a recognizance to heaven,
Binding us over in the courts above,
To plead to the indictment of our crim~s,
That those who 'scape this world should
    suffer there.   *Southern.*

I'll take thy word for faith, not ask thine
    oath;
Who shuns not to break one, will sure
    crack both.   *Shakespeare.*

Obedience.

I hourly learn a doctrine of obedience.
    Shakespeare.

Wicked men obey for fear, but the
good for love.   *Aristotle.*

Let them obey that know not how to
rule.   *Shakespeare.*

Obligation.

An extraordinary haste to discharge an
obligation is a sort of ingratitude.
    La Rochefoucauld.

Observation.

He alone is an acute observer who can
observe minutely without being observed.
    Lavater.

Obstinacy.

Narrowness of mind is often the cause
of obstinacy: we do not easily believe beyond what we see.   *La Rochefoucauld.*

An obstinate man does not hold opinions, but they hold him.   *Pope.*

Stiff opinion, always in the wrong.
    Dryden.

Occasion.

Let me not let pass
Occasion, which now smiles. *Milton.*

Ocean.

Whosoever commands the sea commands the trade; whosoever commands the trade of the world commands the riches of the world, and, consequently, the world itself. *Sir Walter Raleigh.*

Offence.

Who fears t' offend takes the first step to please. *Cibber.*

Offences ought to be pardoned, for few offend willingly, but as they are compelled by some affection. *Hegesippus.*

At every trifle scorn to take offence,
That always shews great pride or little
    sense. *Pope.*

Omissions.

Omissions, no less than commissions, are often times branches of injustice.
            Antoninus.

Opiniators.

There are a sort of men, whose visages
Do cream and mantle, like a standing
    pond;
And do a wilful stillness entertain,
With purpose to be dress'd in an opinion
Of wisdom, gravity, profound conceit;
As who should say, *I am Sir Oracle,
And, when I ope my lips, let no dog bark?*
  . . . I do know of these
That therefore only are reputed wise,
For saying nothing. *Shakespeare.*

Opinion.

Opinion, the blind goddess of fools, foe
To the virtuous, and only friend to
Undeserving persons. *Chapman.*

If a man would register all his opinions upon love, politics, religion, and learning, what a bundle of inconsistencies and contradictions would appear at last! *Swift.*

Opinion, that great fool, makes fools of all. *Field.*

There's nothing good or bad, but thinking makes it so. *Shakespeare.*

Opinion is that high and mighty dame
Which rules the world; and in the mind
    doth frame
Distaste or liking: for in human race,
She makes the fancy various as the face.
    Howel.

Opinions.

He that never changed any of his opinions never corrected any of his mistakes; and he who was never wise enough to find out any mistakes in himself will not be charitable enough to excuse what he reckons mistakes in others.

Opportunity.

There is a tide in the affairs of men,
Which, taken at the flood, leads on to for-
    tune;
Omitted, all the voyage of their life
Is bound in shallows and in miseries:
On such a full sea are we now afloat,
And we must take the current when it
    serves,
Or lose our ventures. *Shakespeare.*

Opportunity has hair in front, behind she is bald; if you seize her by the forelock, you may hold her, but, it suffered to escape, not Jupiter himself can catch her again. *From the Latin.*

There sometimes wants only a stroke of fortune to discover numberless latent good or bad qualities, which would otherwise have been eternally concealed: as words written with a certain liquor appear only when applied to the fire. *Greville.*

Opposed.

Equally to God and truth opposed;
Opposed as darkness to the light of
    heaven. *Pollok.*

Orator.

What the orators want in depth, they give you in length. *Montesquieu.*

Fire in each eye, and papers in each hand,
They rave, recite, and madden round the
   land.   *Pope.*

Order.

Order is the sanity of the mind, the
health of the body, the peace of the city,
the security of the state. As the beams to
a house, as the bones to the microcosm of
man, so is order to all things.   *Southey.*

Order is heaven's first law; and this con-
   fest,
Some are, and must be, greater than the
   rest,
More rich, more wise; but who infers
   from hence
That such are happier, shocks all common
   sense.   *Pope.*

Originality.

The little mind who loves itself, will
write and think with the vulgar; but the
great mind will be bravely eccentric, and
scorn the beaten road, from universal benevolence.   *Goldsmith.*

Orphan.

An orphan's curse would drag to hell
A spirit from on high.   *Coleridge.*

Pain.

Long pains, with use of bearing, are
half eased.   *Dryden.*

Parasite.

Your friend, your pimp, your hanger-on,
   what not?
Your lacquey, but without the shoulder-
   knot.   *Horace.*

Pardon.

Pardon, I beseech Thee, the iniquity of
this people, according unto the greatness
of Thy mercy! And the Lord said I have
pardoned, according to thy word.
                          Numbers xiv, 19.

Thou art a God ready to pardon; gracious and merciful, slow to anger, and of
great kindness.   *Nehemiah* ix, 17.

Parents.

A suspicious parent makes an artful
child.   *Haliburton.*

Parting.

Abruptness is an eloquence in parting, when spinning out the time is but the weaving of new sorrow.

Sir John Suckling.

To die and part
Is a less evil; but to part and live,
There—there's the torment. *Lansdowne.*

Farewell; God knows, when we shall meet again,
I have a faint cold, fear thrills through my veins,
That almost freezes up the heat of life.
Shakespeare.

My heart is heavy at the remembrance of all the miles that lie between us; and I can scarcely believe that you are so distant from me. We are parted; and every parting is a form of death, as every re-union is a type of heaven. *Edwards.*

Good night, good night! parting is such sweet sorrow
That I shall say—good night till it be morrow. *Shakespeare.*

Passion.

How terrible is passion! how our reason
Falls down before it! whilst the tortur'd frame,
Like a ship dash'd by fierce encount'ring tides,
And of her pilot spoil'd, drives round and round,
The sport of wind and wave. *Barford.*

The ruling passion, be it what it will,
The ruling passion conquers reason still.
Pope.

Passions.

Passion often makes a madman of the cleverest man, and renders the greatest fools clever.

The passions are the only orators that always persuade.

The passions often engender their contraries. *La Rochefoucauld.*

Passions, like seas, will have their ebbs and flows. *Lee.*

The wither'd frame, the ruin'd mind,
The wreck by passion left behind;
A shrivell'd scroll, a scatter'd leaf,
Sear'd by the autumn-blast of grief.
Byron.

Our passions are like convulsion fits,
which, though they make us stronger for
a time, leave us the weaker ever after.
Pope.

The passions, like heavy bodies down
steep hills, once in motion, move themselves, and know no ground but the bottom. *Fuller.*

Oh! she has passions which outstrip the
wind,
And tear her virtue up, as tempests root
the sea. *Congreve.*

Patience.

If the wicked flourish, and thou suffer,
be not discouraged. They are fatted for
destruction: thou art dieted for health.
Fuller.

Patience is sorrow's salve. *Churchill.*

There is a limit at which forbearance
ceases to be a virtue. *Burke.*

He that would have a cake out of the
wheat must tarry the grinding.
Shakespeare.

Patriot.

Who, firmly good in a corrupted state,
Against the rage of tyrants singly stood,
Invincible. *Thomson.*

'Tis home-felt pleasure prompts the patri-
ot's sigh
This makes him wish to live, and dare to
die. *Campbell.*

Peace.

Down the dark future, through long gen-
erations,
The echoing sounds grow fainter and then
cease;
And like a bell, with solemn, sweet vi-
brations,
I hear once more the voice of Christ say
"Peace!" *Longfellow.*

Peace hath her victories,
No less renown'd than war.   *Milton.*

Peacemakers.

Blessed are the peacemakers, for they
shall be called the children of God.
St. Matthew v, 9.

Pedantry.

Brimful of learning, see that pedant
stride,
Bristling with horrid Greek, and puff'd
with pride!
A thousand authors he in vain has read,
And with their maxims stuff'd his empty
head;
And thinks that without Aristotle's rule,
Reason is blind, and common sense a
fool!   *Boileau.*

Pedantry crams our heads with learned
lumber, and takes out our brains to make
room for it.   *Colton.*

Pen.

Oh! nature's noblest gift—my grey goose
quill:
Slave of my thoughts, obedient to my
will,
Torn from thy parent bird to form a pen,
That mighty instrument of little men!
Byron.

Penetration.

The balls of sight are so formed, that
one man's eyes are spectacles to another,
to read his heart within.   *Johnson.*

Penury.

Chill penury weighs down the heart, itself; and though it sometimes be endured
with calmness, it is but the calmness of
despair.   *Mrs. Jameson.*

People.

The world may be divided into people
that read, people that write, people that
think, and fox hunters.   *Shenstone.*

Perfection.

To arrive at perfection, a man should have very sincere friends or inveterate enemies; because he would be made sensible of his good or ill conduct, either by the censures of the one, or the admonitions of the other.   *Diogenes.*

Perseverance.

Yet I argue not
Against heaven's hand or will, nor bate a
    jot
Of heart or hope, but still bear up and
    steer
Right onward.   *Milton.*

When I take the humor of a thing once, I am like your tailor's needle—I go through.   *Ben Jonson.*

By gnawing through a dyke even a rat may drown a nation.   *Edward Burke.*

Let us only suffer any person to tell us his story morning and evening, but for one twelve-month, and he will become our master.   *Burke.*

Perseverance and Obstinacy.

The difference between perseverance and obstinancy is that one often comes from a strong will, and the other from a strong won't.

Perversity.

Some men put me in mind of half-bred horses. which often grow worse in proportion as you feed and exercise them for improvement.   *Greville.*

Philosophy.

Philosophy, when superficially studied, excites doubt; when thoroughly explored, it dispels it.   *Bacon.*

A little philosophy inclineth man's mind to atheism, but depth of philosophy bringeth a man's mind about to religion.
                    Bacon.

Do not all charms fly,
At the mere touch of cold philosophy?
                    Keats.

Physicians.

If you need a physician, employ these three—a cheerful mind, rest, and a temperate diet.

The patient can oftener do without the doctor, than the doctor without the patient. *Zimmerman.*

Physiognomy.

As the language of the face is universal, so 'tis very comprehensive; no laconism can reach it: 'tis the short hand of the mind, and crowds a great deal in a little room. *Jeremy Collier.*

Picture.

A picture is a poem without words.
Horace.

Pity.

The truly brave are soft of heart and eyes,
And feel for what their duty bids them
    do. *Byron.*

No radiant pearl which crested fortune
    wears,
No gem that, twinkling, hangs from beauty's ears,
Not the bright stars which night's blue
    arch adorn,
Nor rising suns that gild the vernal morn,
Shine with such lustre as the tear that
    breaks
For other's woe, down virtue's manly
    cheeks. *Darwin.*

Villain, thou know'st no law of God or
    man;
No beast so fierce, but knows some touch
    of pity. *Shakespeare.*

Plagiarism.

It is one thing to purloin finely-tempered steel, and another to take a pound of literary old iron, and convert it in the furnace of one's mind into a hundred watchsprings, worth each a thousand times as much as the iron. When genius borrows, it borrows grandly, giving to the borrowed matter, a life and beauty it lacked before. *Anon.*

Pleasure.

The seeds of repentance are sown in youth by pleasure, but the harvest is reaped in age by pain.   *Colton.*

Enjoy your present pleasures so as not to injure those that are to follow.
                             Seneca.

Flowers are like the pleasures of the world.   *Shakespeare.*

Pleasure soon exhausts us and itself also; but endeavor never does.   *Richter.*

Pleasure, or wrong or rightly understood, Our greatest evil, or our greatest good.
                             Pope.

Pleasure that comes unlooked for is thrice welcome.   *Rogers.*

Why, all delights are vain; but that most vain,
Which, with pain purchas'd, doth inherit pain.   *Shakespeare.*

Pleasures.

Choose such pleasures as recreate much, and cost little.   *Fuller.*

Put only the restriction on your pleasures—be cautious that they hurt no creature that has life.   *Zimmerman.*

Venture not to the utmost bounds of even lawful pleasure; the limits of good and evil join.   *Fuller.*

It is sad
To think how few our pleasures really are:
And for the which we risk eternal good.
                             Bailey.

Poet.

Just writes to make his barrenness appear,
And strain from hard-bound brains, eight lines a year.   *Pope.*

Poet! esteem thy noble part,
    Still listen, still record,
Sacred historian of the heart,
    And moral nature's lord.
        Richard M. Milnes.

Poetry.

Poetry is the eloquence of truth.
Campbell.

Poetry has been to me "its own exceeding great reward;" it has soothed my afflictions; it has multiplied and refined my enjoyments; it has endeared solitude; and it has given me the habit of wishing to discover the good and the beautiful in all that meets and surrounds me.
Coleridge.

Poets.

Poets are all who love—who feel great truths—
And tell them.
Bailey.

Policy.

The devil knew not what he did, when he made man politic.
Shakespeare.

Politeness.

As charity covers a multitude of sins before God, so does politeness before men.
Chesterfield.

When two goats met on a bridge which was too narrow to allow either to pass or return, the goat which lay down that the other might walk over it, was a finer gentleman than Lord Chesterfield.
Cecil.

Politician.

A politician, Proteus-like must alter
His face, and habit; and, like water, seem
Of the same color that the vessel is
That doth contain it; varying his form
With the chameleon at each object's change.
Mason.

Politics.

Who's in or out, who moves the grand machine,
Nor stirs my curiosity, or spleen;
Secrets of state no more I wish to know
Than secret movements of a puppet-show;
Let but the puppets move, I've my desire,
Unseen the hand which guides the master wire.
Churchill.

Popularity.

He who can listen pleas'd to such applause,
Buys at a dearer rate than I dare purchase,
And pays for idle air with sense and virtue.   *Mallett.*

Oh, popular applause, what heart of man
Is proof against thy sweet seducing
charms?
The wisest and the best feel urgent need
Of all their caution in thy gentlest gales:
But swelled into a dust—who then, alas!
With all his canvas set, and inexpert,
And therefore heedless, can withstand thy
power.   *Cowper.*

Please not thyself the flattering crowd to
hear;
'Tis fulsome stuff, to please thy itching
ear.
Survey thy soul, not what thou dost appear,
But what thou art.   *Persius.*

Possibilities.

To him nothing is impossible, who is always dreaming of his past possibilities.
                                        Carlyle.

Poverty.

It is not poverty so much as pretence
that harasses a ruined man—the struggle
between a proud mind and an empty
purse—the keeping up a hollow show that
must soon come to an end. Have the
courage to appear poor, and you disarm
poverty of its sharpest sting.
                                Mrs. Jameson.

O blissful poverty!
Nature, too partial to thy lot, assigns
Health, freedom, innocence, and downy
peace,
Her real goods; and only mocks the great
With empty pageantries.   *Fenton.*

This mournful truth is everywhere con-
ͻ fessed,
Slow rises worth by poverty depressed.
                                     Johnson.

He is poor whose expenses exceed his income. *La Bruyère.*

To mortal men great loads allotted be;
But of all packs no pack like poverty.
Herrick.

Poverty makes people satirical,—soberly, sadly, bitterly satirical. *Friswell.*

Power.

Nothing, indeed, but the possession of some power can with any certainty discover what at the bottom is the true character of any man. *Burke.*

Even in war, moral power is to physical as three parts out of four. *Napoleon I.*

Praise.

Let another man praise thee, and not thine own mouth; a stranger, and not thine own lips. *Proverbs* xxvii, 2.

Allow no man to be so free with you as to praise you to your face. Your vanity by this means will want its food. At the same time your passion for esteem will be more fully gratified; men will praise you in their actions: where you now receive one compliment, you will then receive twenty civilities. *Steele.*

Praise was originally a pension, paid by the world. *Swift.*

Those men who are commended by everybody, must be very extraordinary men; or, which is more probable, very inconsiderable men. *Greville.*

It gives me pleasure to be praised by you whom all men praise. *Tully.*

The more you speak of yourself, the more you are likely to lie. *Zimmerman.*

There's not one wise man among twenty will praise himself. *Shakespeare.*

Prayer.

If any of you lack wisdom, let him ask of God, that giveth to all men liberally and upbraideth not; and it shall be given him. But let him ask in faith, nothing wavering. *James* i, 5, 6.

God is a spirit: and they that worship
Him, must worship Him in spirit and in
truth.   *St. John* iv, 24.

Ye ask, and receive not, because ye ask
amiss.   *James* iv, 3.

He that cometh to God, must believe
that He is, and that He is a rewarder of
them that diligently seek Him.
                                Heb. xi, 6.

Fountain of mercy! whose pervading eye
Can look within and read what passes
    there,
Accept my thoughts for thanks; I have no
    words.
My soul o'erfraught with gratitude, re-
    jects
The aid of language—Lord!—behold my
    heart.   *Hannah More.*

Prayer purifies; it is a self-preached
sermon.   *Richter.*

Any heart turned Godward, feels more
    joy
In one short hour of prayer, than e'er was
    rais'd
By all the feasts on earth since their
    foundation.   *Bailey.*

More things are wrought by prayer
Than this world dreams of.
                                Tennyson.

In prayer it is better to have a heart
without words, than words without a
heart.   *Bunyan.*

Is not prayer a study of truth—a sally
of the soul into the unfound infinite? No
man ever prayed heartily without learning
something; but when a faithful thinker
resolute to detach every object from per-
sonal relations, and see it in the light of
thought, shall, at the same time, kindle
science with the fire of the holiest affections, then will God go forth anew into
the creation.   *Emerson.*

Let prayer be the key of the morning
and the bolt of the evening.
                                Matthew Henry.

179

Prejudice.

To divest one's self of some prejudices, would be like taking off the skin to feel the better. *Greville.*

Press.

"The Press!" all lands shall sing;
The press, the press we bring
    All lands to bless.
O pallid Want! O Labor stark!
Behold, we bring the second ark!
    The press! the press! the press!
Ebenezer Elliott.

Presumption.

Fools rush in where angels fear to tread. *Pope.*

Pretension.

Where there is much pretension, much has been borrowed; nature never pretends. *Lavater.*

It is no disgrace not to be able to do everything; but to undertake, or pretend to do, what you are not made for, is not only shameful, but extremely troublesome and vexatious. *Plutarch.*

Pride.

The lofty pine is oftenest agitated by the winds—high towers rush to the earth with a heavier fall—and the lightning most frequently strikes the highest mountains. *Horace.*

What is pride? a whizzing rocket
That would emulate a star.
Wordsworth.

Pride that dines on vanity, sups on contempt. *B. Franklin.*

He whose pride oppresses the humble may, perhaps, be humbled, but will never be humble. *Lavater.*

Defeated, but not dismayed,—crushed to the earth, but not humiliated,—he seemed to grow more haughty beneath disaster, and to experience a fierce satisfaction in draining the last dregs of bitterness. *Washington Irving.*

When pride begins, love ceases.
Lavater.

The vile are only vain; the great are proud.
Byron.

Principles.

Let us cling to our principles as the mariner clings to his last plank when night and tempest close around him.
And oftener changed their principles than their shirts.
Dr. Young.

Prison.

A felon's cell—
The fittest earthly type of hell!
Whittier.

Emblem of hell, nursery of vice.
Tom Brown.

Procrastination.

Procrastination is the thief of time.
Dr. Young.

Defer not till to-morrow to be wise,
To-morrow's sun to thee may never rise.
Congreve.

Progress.

Living movement.
Carlyle.
The goal of yesterday will be the starting point of to-morrow.
Carlyle.

Promises.

He who is most slow in making a promise, is the most faithful in the performance of it.
Rousseau.

Prosperity.

Take care to be an economist in prosperity; there is no fear of your not being one in adversity.
Zimmerman.

Knaves will thrive,
When honest plainness knows not how to live.
Shirley.

Whilst you are prosperous you can number many friends; but when the storm comes you are left alone.
Ovid.

Proverbs.

The wisdom of many, and the wit of one.
Lord John Russell.

> Jewels five-words long,
> That on the stretch'd forefinger of all
> time
> Sparkle forever.   *Tennyson.*

Providence.

The ways of heaven are dark and intri-
cate,
Puzzled in mazes, and perplex'd with er-
rors;
Our understanding traces them in vain,
Lost and bewilder'd in the fruitless
search;
Nor sees with how much art the windings
run,
Nor where the regular confusion ends.
       Addison.

How just is Providence in all its works.
How swift to overtake us in our crimes!
       Lansdowne.

Prudence.

Men are born with two eyes, but with
one tongue, in order that they should see
twice as much as they say.   *Colton.*

Want of prudence is too frequently the
want of virtue; nor is there on earth a
more powerful advocate for vice than poverty?   *Goldsmith.*

Punishment.

Let rules be fix'd that may our rage contain,
And punish faults with a proportion'd
pain;
And do not flay him, who deserves alone
A whipping for the fault that he has
done.   *Horace.*

The seeds of our punishment are sown
at the same time we commit sin.
       Hesiod.

Purity.

An angel might have stoop'd to see,
And bless'd her for her purity.
       Dr. Mackay.

Purity is the feminine, truth the mascu-
line, of honor.   *Hare.*

Purse.

Their love
Lies in their purses; and whoso empties
them,
By so much fills their hearts with deadly
hate. *Shakespeare.*

Quarrels.

Those who in quarrels interpose,
Must often wipe a bloody nose. *Gay.*

If he had two ideas in his head, they
would fall out with each other.
Johnson.

I consider your very testy and quarrel-
some people in the same light as I do a
loaded gun, which may, by accident, go off
and kill one. *Shenstone.*

Quotations.

Some for renown on scraps of learning
dote
And think they grow immortal as they
quote.
To patchwork learn'd quotations are al-
lied,
But strive to make our poverty our pride.
Young.

I am but a gatherer, and a disposer of
other men's stuff. *Watton.*

If the world like it not, so much the
worse for them. *Cowper.*

Rabble.

They condemn what they do not understand. *Cicero.*

A hundred mouths, a hundred tongues,
And throats of brass, inspired with iron
lungs. *Virgil.*

Rage.

They could neither of 'em speak for
rage and so fell a sputtering at one
another like two roasting apples.
Congreve.

My rage is not malicious; like a spark
Of fire by steel inforced out of a flint.
It is no sooner kindled, but extinct.
Goffe.

183

Rain.

How beautiful is the rain!
After the dust and heat,
In the broad and fiery street,
In the narrow lane;
How beautiful is the rain!
How it clatters along the roofs,
Like the tramp of hoofs;
How it gushes and struggles out
From the throat of the overflowing
    spout.   *Longfellow.*

Dashing in big drops on the narrow pane,
  And making mournful music for the
    mind,
While plays his interlude the wizard
    wind,
I hear the singing of the frequent rain.
    Wm. H. Burleigh.

Rainbow.

How glorious is thy girdle cast,
  O'er mountain, tower, and town;
Or mirror'd in the ocean vast,
  A thousand fathoms down.   *Campbell.*

  That gracious thing, made up of tears
and light.   *Coleridge.*

What skillful limner e'er would choose
To paint the rainbow's various hues,
Unless to mortal it were given
To dip his brush in dyes of heaven?
    Scott.

Rank.

The rank is but the guinea's stamp,
The man's the gowd for a' that.   *Burns.*

Rant.

    Nay, an' thou 'lt mouth,
I'll rant as well as thou.   *Shakespeare.*

Rapture.

Not the poet in the moment
Fancy lightens on his e'e,
Kens the pleasure, feels the rapture
That thy presence gi'es to me.   *Burns.*

Rascals.

  Make yourself an honest man, and then
you may be sure that there is one rascal
less in the world.   *Carlyle.*

Rashness.

That's a valiant flea that dare eat his breakfast on the lip of a lion.

Shakespeare.

Reading.

As a man may be eating all day, and for want of digestion is never nourished, so these endless readers may cram themselves in vain with intellectual food.

Dr. I. Watts.

Read not to contradict and confute, nor to believe and take for granted, nor to find talk and discourse,—but to weigh and consider. *Bacon.*

To read without reflecting, is like eating without digesting. *Burke.*

Reason.

He who will not reason, is a bigot; he who cannot, is a fool; and he who dares not, is a slave. *Byron.*

When a man has not a good reason for doing a thing, he has one good reason for letting it alone. *Sir Walter Scott.*

One can never repeat too often, that reason, as it exists in man, is only our intellectual eye, and that, like the eye, to see, it needs light,—to see clearly and far, it needs the light of heaven. *Anon.*

Reason is the test of ridicule—not ridicule the test of truth. *Warburton.*

Neither great poverty, nor great riches, will hear reason. *Fielding.*

Reckoning.

I am ill at reckoning; it fits the spirit of a tapster. *Shakespeare.*

So comes a reck'ning when the banquet's
    o'er,
The dreadful reck'ning and men smile no
    more. *Gay.*

Recreation.

Amusements to virtue are like breezes of air to the flame—gentle ones will fan it, but strong ones will put it out.

David Thomas.

Refinement.

That only can with propriety be styled refinement which, by strengthening the intellect, purifies the manners.   *Coleridge.*

Reflection.

There is one art of which man should be master,—the art of reflection.
Coleridge.

Reform.

Reform, like charity, must begin at home. Once well at home, how will it radiate outwards, irrepressible, into all that we touch and handle, speak and work; kindling every new light by incalculable contagion, spreading, in geometric ratio, far and wide, doing good only wherever it spreads, and not evil.   *Carlyle.*

He who reforms himself, has done more towards reforming the public, than a crowd of noisy, impotent patriots.   *Lavater.*

Regularity.

Regularity is unity, unity is godlike, only the devil is changeable.   *Richter.*

Religion.

Religion is the best armor that a man can have, but it is the worst cloak.
Bunyan.

True religion
Is always mild, propitious, and humble,
Plays not the tyrant, plants no faith in
    blood;
Nor bears destruction on her chariot-
    wheels;
But stoops to polish, succor, and redress,
And builds her grandeur on the public
    good.   *Miller.*

Genuine religion is not so much a matter of feeling as of principle.

An atheist is but a mad ridiculous derider of piety; but a hypocrite makes a sober jest of God and religion; he finds it easier to be upon his knees than to rise to a good action.   *Pope.*

Men will wrangle for religion; write for it; fight for it; die for it; anything but—
live for it. *Colton.*

Measure not men by Sundays, without regarding what they do all the week after.
Fuller.

I have lived long enough to know what I did not at one time believe—that no society can be upheld in happiness and honor without the sentiment of religion.
La Place.

Pure religion and undefiled before God and the Father is this: To visit the fatherless and widows in their affliction, and to keep himself unspotted from the world.
James i, 27.

For in religion as in friendship, they who profess most are ever the least sincere.
Sheridan.

A man devoid of religion, is like a horse without a bridle. *From the Latin.*

Remembrance.

Let never day nor night unhallow'd pass,
But still remember what the Lord has done. *Shakespeare.*

Remorse.

Remorse is the echo of a lost virtue.
Bulwer Lytton.

One of those terrible moments when the wheel of passion stands suddenly still.
Bulwer Lytton.

Repentance.

Repentance,
A salve, a comfort, and a cordial;
He that hath her, the keys of heaven hath:
This is the guide, this is the post, the path.
Drayton.

Repose.

Our foster-nurse of nature is repose.
Shakespeare.

When a man finds not repose in himself it is in vain for him to seek it elsewhere.
From the French.

Reproof.

Forbear sharp speeches to her; she's a
   lady,
So tender of rebukes that words are
   strokes,
And strokes death to her.   *Shakespeare.*

Reputation.

O reputation! dearer far than life,
Thou precious balsam, lovely, sweet of
   smell,
Whose cordial drops once split by some
   rash hand,
Not all the owner's care, nor the repenting
   toil
Of the rude spiller, ever can collect
To its first purity and native sweetness.
                           Sir W. Raleigh.

How many people live on the reputation
of the reputation they might have made!
                           Holmes.

How difficult it is to save the bark of
reputation from the rocks of ignorance.
                           Petrarch.

Thy credit wary keep, 'tis quickly gone:
Being got by many actions, lost by one.
                           Randolph.

The reputation of a man is like his
shadow: It sometimes follows and sometimes precedes him, it is sometimes longer
and sometimes shorter than his natural
size.   *French Proverb.*

Resignation.

         Whate'er my doom;
It cannot be unhappy: God hath given me
The boon of resignation.   *Wilson.*

It is the Lord: let Him do what seem-
eth Him good.   *Samuel* iii, 18.

The Lord gave, and the Lord hath taken
away; blessed be the name of the Lord.
                           Job i, 21.

Rest.

Rest is the sweet sauce of labor.
                           Plutarch.

Alternate rest and labor long endure.
                           Ovid.

Retreat.

In all the trade of war, no feat
Is nobler than a brave retreat.
Butler

Retribution.

Man never fastened one end of a chain
around the neck of his brother, that God's
own hand did not fasten the other end
round the neck of the oppressor.
Lamartine.

And thus the whirligig of time brings in
his revenges. *Shakespeare.*

Revenge.

How rash, how inconsiderate is rage!
How wretched, oh! how fatal is our error,
When to revenge precipitate we run;
Revenge, that still with double force re-
coils
Back on itself, and is its own revenge,
While to the short liv'd, momentary joy,
Succeeds a train of woes, an age of tor-
ments. *Frowde.*

The best sort of revenge is not to be like
him who did the injury. *Antoninus.*

Rhetoric.

The heart's still rhetoric, disclosed with
eyes. *Shakespeare.*

Rhyme and Reason.

I was promised on a time,
To have reason for my rhyme;
From that time until this season,
I received no rhyme nor reason.
Spenser.

Riches.

And his best riches, ignorance of wealth.
Goldsmith.

As riches and favor forsake a man, we
discover him to be a fool, but nobody
could find it out in his prosperity.
La Bruyère.

He hath riches sufficient, who hath
enough to be charitable.
Sir Thomas Browne.

A great fortune is a great slavery.
Seneca.

Believe not much them that seem to despise riches; for they despise them that
despair of them; and none are worse when
they come to them. Be not penny-wise;
riches have wings, and sometimes they fly
away of themselves, sometimes they must
be set flying to bring in more. *Bacon.*

Rich, be not exalted; poor, be not de-
jected. *Cleobulus.*

Ridicule.

If ridicule were employed to laugh men
out of vice and folly, it might be of some
use; but it is made use of to laugh men
out of virtue and good sense, by attacking
everything solemn and serious. *Addison.*

Ring.

Oh! how many torments lie in the small
circle of a wedding ring. *Colley Cibber.*

Rivalry.

Two stars keep not motion in one sphere.
Shakespeare.

Roaring.

I will roar, that it will do any man's
heart good to hear me.

I will aggravate my voice so, that I will
roar you as gently as any suckling dove; I
will roar you an 'twere any nightingale.
Shakespeare.

Rod.

Take thy correction mildly. Kiss the
rod. *Shakespeare.*

He that spareth his rod hateth his son.
Proverbs xiii, 24.

Rudeness.

A man has no more right to say an uncivil thing, than to act one; no more right
to say a rude thing to another, than to
knock him down. *Johnson.*

Rumor.

The flying rumors gather'd as they roll'd
Scarce any tale was sooner heard than told,
And all who told it added something new,
And all who heard it made enlargement,
    too,
In every ear it spread, on every tongue it
    grew.   *Pope.*

Sabbath.

The poor man's day.   *Grahame.*

The Sabbath was made for man, and
not man for the Sabbath.   *St. Mark* ii, 27.

Sailor.

I love the sailor; his eventful life—
His generous spirit—his contempt of dan-
    ger—
His firmness in the gale, the wreck, the
    strife;
And though a wild and reckless ocean-
    ranger,
God grant he make the port, when life is
    o'er,
Where storms are hush'd, and billows
    break no more   *Walter Colton.*

Satan.

Th' infernal serpent; he it was, whose
    guile,
Stirr'd up with envy and revenge, deceiv'd
The mother of mankind.   *Milton.*

Here we may reign secure; and in my
    choice
To reign is worth ambition, though in hell.
Better to reign in hell than serve in heaven.
          Milton.

Satiety.

A surfeit of the sweetest things,
The deepest loathing to the stomach brings.
          Shakespeare.

Satire.

Wit larded with malice.
          Shakespeare.

A bitter jest, when the satire comes too
near the truth, leaves a sharp sting behind.
          Tacitus.

Scandal.

Nor do they trust their tongues alone,
But speak a language of their own;
Can read a nod, a shrug, a look,
Far better than a printed book;
Convey a libel in a frown,
And wink a reputation down;
Or, by the tossing of a fan,
Describe the lady and the man.   *Swift.*

Scar.

A scar nobly got is a good livery of
honor.   *Shakespeare.*

Scepticism.

I would rather dwell in the dim fog of
superstition than in air rarified to nothing
by the air pump of unbelief; in which the
panting breast expires, vainly and convul-
sively gasping for breath.   *Richter.*

Schemes.

The best laid schemes o' mice an' men,
    Gang aft agley,
And lea'e us nought but grief and pain,
    For promised joy.   *Burns.*

Scorn.

Oh! what a thing, ye gods, is scorn or
    pity!
Heap on me, Heaven, the heat of all man-
    kind,
Load me with envy, malice, detestation;
Let me be horrid to all apprehension;
Let the world shun me, so I 'scape but
    scorn.   *Lee.*

Sculpture.

A statue lies hid in a block of marble;
and the art of the statuary only clears
away the superfluous matter, and removes
the rubbish.   *Addison.*

Sea.

Praise the sea, but keep on land.
                    Geo. Herbert.

Secret.

'Tis in my memory lock'd,
And you yourself shall keep the key of it.
                    Shakespeare.

> A secret in his mouth,
> Is like a wild bird put into a cage;
> Whose door no sooner opens, but 'tis out.
> *Jonsoil.*

Generally he perceived in men of devout simplicity this opinion; that the secrets of nature were the secrets of God, part of that glory into which man is not to press too boldly.   *Bacon.*

Self.

And though all cry down self, none means
His ownself in a literal sense.   *Butler.*

Be always displeased with what thou art, if thou desirest to attain to what thou art not; for where thou hast pleased thyself, there thou abidest. But if thou sayest I have enough, thou perishest. Always add, always walk, always proceed. Neither stand still, nor go back, nor deviate.
Augustine.

Self-Confidence.

For they can conquer who believe they can.   *Virgil.*

Self-Control.

He who reigns within himself, and rules passions, desires and fears, is more than a king.   *Milton.*

Self-Deception.

No man was ever so much deceived by another as by himself.   *Greville.*

Self-Defense.

Self-defense is nature's eldest law.
Dryden.

Self-Help.

Help yourself, and Heaven will help you.
La Fontaine.

I have ever held it as a maxim, never to do that through another, which it was possible for me to execute myself.
Montesquieu.

Self-Love.

Self-love is more cunning than the most cunning man in the world.
La Rochefoucauld.

Self-love is the greatest of flatterers.
La Rochefoucauld.

Of all mankind, each loves himself the best. *Terence.*

Self-Respect.

The reverence of a man's self is, next religion, the chiefest bridle of all vices.
Lord Bacon.

Sense.

Something there is more needful than expense,
And something previous e'en to taste—'tis sense :
Good sense which only is the gift of heaven,
And though no science, fairly worth the seven. *Pope.*

Sensibility.

The heart that is soonest awake to the flowers,
Is always the first to be touch'd by the thorns. *Moore.*

Servant.

Master, go on, and I will follow thee
To the last gasp, with truth and loyalty.
Shakespeare.

If thou hast a loitering servant, send him of thy errand just before his dinner.
Fuller.

Services.

The daisy, by the shadow that it casts,
Protects the ling'ring dewdrop from the sun. *Wordsworth.*

Shame.

It is the guilt, not the scaffold, which constitutes the shame. *Corneille.*

Shaving.

Men for their sins
Have shaving, too, entail'd upon their chins. *Byron.*

Ship.

She comes majestic with her swelling sails,
The gallant bark; along her watery way
Homeward she drives before the favoring
    gales;
Now flirting at their length the streamers
    play,
And now they ripple with the ruffling
    breeze.   *Southey.*

Silence.

The temple of our purest thoughts is—
silence!   *Mrs. Hale.*

Fellows who have no tongues are often
all eyes and ears.   *Haliburton.*

Let us be silent, that we may hear the
whispers of the gods.   *Emerson.*

Simplicity.

Whose nature is so far from doing harm,
That he suspects none.   *Shakespeare.*

Sin.

He that falls into sin is a man; that
grieves at it may be a saint; that boasteth
of it is a devil.   *Fuller.*
Few love to hear the sins they love to act.
          Shakespeare.

Sincerity.

The more honesty a man has, the less he
affects the air of a saint. The affectation
of sanctity is a blotch on the face of piety.
          Lavater.

Sincerity is like traveling in a plain
beaten road, which commonly brings a
man sooner to his journey's end than by-
ways, in which men often lose themselves.
          Tillotson.

Skull.

Where be your gibes now? your gambols? your songs? your flashes of merri-
ment that were wont to set the table on a
roar?   *Shakespeare.*

Slander.

Slander—
Whose edge is sharper than the sword.
          Shakespeare.

Slander meets no regard from noble minds;
Only the base believe, what the base only
  utter.   *Beller.*

Slanderers.

Long-breath'd talkers, minion lispers,
Cutting honest throats by whispers. *Scott.*

Sleep.

Sleep, that knits up the ravell'd sleeve of
  care;
The death of each day's life, sore labor's
  bath.
Balm of hurt minds, great Nature's second
  course,
Chief nourisher in life's feast.
                              Shakespeare.

  Downy sleep, death's counterfeit.
                              Shakespeure.

  How wonderful is death, death and his
brother, sleep!   *Shelley.*
O magic sleep! O comfortable bird,
That broodest o'er the troubled sea of the
  mind
Till it is hush'd and smooth! O unconfin'd
Restraint! imprison'd liberty! great key
To golden palaces—ay, all the world
Of silvery enchantment!   *Keats.*

Sneer.

There was a laughing devil in his sneer,
That raised emotions both of rage and
  fear,
And where his frown of hatred darkly fell.
Hope, withering, fled, and mercy sighed
  farewell.   *Byron.*
  A habit of sneering, marks the egotist,
or the fool, or the knave, or all three.
                              Lavater.

Society.

  Society is like a lawn, where every
roughness is smoothed, every bramble erad-
icated, and where the eye is delighted by
the smiling verdure of a velvet surface.
He, however, who would study nature in
its wildness and variety, must plunge into
the forest, must explore the glen, must
stem the torrent, and dare the precipice.
                       Washington Irving.

Solitude.

Alone on a wide, wide sea,
So lonely 'twas, that God himself
Scarce seemed there to be.   *Coleridge.*

Oh, lost to virtue—lost to manly thought,
Lost to the noble sallies of the soul!
Who think it solitude to be alone. *Young.*

The thought,
The deadly thought of solitude.   *Keats.*

Sorrow.

When sorrows come, they come not single
    spies,
But in battalions!   *Shakespeare.*

Any mind that is capable of a *real sorrow* is capable of good.   *Mrs. Stowe.*

Sorrow seems sent for our instruction,
as we darken the cages of birds when we
would teach them to sing.   *Richter.*

The first sharp sorrow—ay, the breaking up
Of that deep fountain, ne'er to be seal'd
Till we with time close up the great ac-
    count.   *Caroline Bowles.*

Soul.

Alas! while the body stands so broad
and brawny, must the soul lie blinded,
dwarfed, stupefied, almost annihilated?
Alas! this was, too, a breath of God, bestowed in heaven, but on earth never to be
unfolded!   *Carlyle.*

There are souls which fall from heaven
like flowers, but ere they bloom are crushed
under the foul tread of some brutal hoof.
      Richter.

Speaking.

Speak but little and well, if you would
be esteemed as a man of merit. *Trench.*

Speech.

A sentence well couched takes both the
sense and the understanding. I love not
those cart-rope speeches that are longer
than the memory of man can fathom.
      Feltham.

Spite.

Spite is a little word but it represents as strange a jumble of feelings and compound of discords, as any polysyllable in the language. *Dickens.*

Spoon.

He must have a long spoon that must eat with the devil. *Shakespeare.*

Spring.

Wide flush the fields; the softening air is balm;
Echo the mountains round; the forest smiles;
And every sense and every heart is joy.
Thomson.

Stars.

There they stand,
Shining in order like a living hymn
Written in light. *Willis.*
The stars hang bright above,
Silent, as if they watch'd the sleeping earth. *Coleridge.*
Those gold candles fix'd in heaven's air.
Shakespeare.

Stoicism.

To feel for none is the true social art
Of the world's stoics—men without a heart. *Byron.*

Story-Telling.

I cannot tell how the truth may be;
I say the tale as 'twas said to me.
Sir Walter Scott.

Study.

Much study is a weariness of the flesh.
Ecclesiastes xii, 12.

Success.

'Tis not in mortals to command success;
But we'll do more, Sempronius.—We'll deserve it. *Addison.*
It is success that colors all in life;
Success makes fools admir'd, makes villains honest,
All the proud virtue of this vaunting world
Fawns on success and power, howe'er acquired. *Thomson.*

Suicide.

Child of despair, and suicide my name.
Savage.

Self-murder, that infernal crime,
Which all the gods level their thunder at!
Fanc.

Sun.

The glorious lamp of heaven, the sun.
Herrick.

Open the casement, and up with the sun!
His gallant journey has now begun,
Over the hills his chariot is roll'd,
Banner'd with glory and burnish'd with
gold;
Over the hills he comes sublime,
Bridegroom of earth, and brother of time!
Martin F. Tupper.

Sunrise.

And see—the sun himself! on wings
Of glory up the east he springs.
Angel of light! who from the time
Those heavens began their march sublime,
Hath first of all the starry choir
Trod in his Maker's steps of fire! *Moore.*

Sunset.

See the descending sun,
Scatt'ring his beams about him as he sinks,
And gilding heaven above, and seas be-
neath,
With paint no mortal pencil can express.
Hopkins.

Superstition.

Superstition renders a man a fool, and
scepticism makes him mad. *Fielding.*

Suspense.

It is a miserable thing to live in sus-
pense, it is the life of the spider. *Swift.*

Suspicion.

It is hardly possible to suspect another
without having in one's self the seeds of
baseness the party is accused of.
Stanislaus.

Swearing.

Swear not at all: neither by heaven; for it is God's throne: nor by the earth; for it is his footstool: neither by Jerusalem; for it is the city of the great king. Neither shalt thou swear by thy head, because thou canst not make one hair white or black. But let your communication be yea, yea; nay, nay: for whatsoever is more than these cometh of evil.   *St. Matthew.*

Tact.

Never join with your friend when he abuses his horse or his wife, unless the one is about to be sold, and the other to be buried.   *Colton.*

Talents.

It seems that nature has concealed at the bottom of our minds, talents and abilities of which we are not aware. The passions alone have the privilege of bringing them to light, and of giving us sometimes views more certain and more perfect than art could possibly produce.

La Rochefoucauld.

Talkers.

As empty vessels make the loudest sound, so they that have the least wit are the greatest babblers.   *Plato.*

Talkers are no good doers. *Shakespeare.*

Talking.

Words learned by rote a parrot may rehearse,
But talking is not always to converse;
Not more distinct from harmony divine,
The constant creaking of a country sign.

Cowper.

Does a man speak foolishly?—suffer him gladly, for you are wise. Does he speak erroneously?—stop such a man's mouth with sound words that cannot be gainsaid. Does he speak truly?—rejoice in the truth.   *Oliver Cromwell.*

Taste.

May not taste be compared to that exquisite sense of the bee, which instantly discovers and extracts the quintessence of every flower, and disregards all the rest of it.   *Greville.*

Tea.

Tea! thou soft, thou sober sage, and venerable liquid;—thou female tongue-running, smile-smoothing, heart-opening, wink-tippling cordial, to whose glorious insipidity I owe the happiest moments of my life, let me fall prostrate! *Colley Cibber.*

Tears.

Beauty's tears are lovelier than her smile.
                              Campbell.
The safety-valves of the heart, when too much pressure is laid on.   *Albert Smith.*
The tears of penitents are the wine of angels   *St. Bernard.*

Temper.

A sunny temper gilds the edges of life's blackest cloud.   *Guthrie.*

Temptation.

He who has no mind to trade with the devil, should be so wise as to keep from his shop.   *South.*
            'Tis one thing to be tempted,
Another thing to fall.   *Shakespeare.*

Testimony and Argument.

Testimony is like an arrow shot from a long bow; the force of it depends on the strength of the hand that draws it. Argument is like an arrow from a cross-bow, which has equal force though shot by a child.   *Bacon.*

Thinkers.

There are very few original thinkers in the world; the greatest part of those who are called philosophers have adopted the opinions of some who went before them.
                    Dugald Stewart.

Thought.

There's too much abstract willing, purpos-
  ing,
In this poor world. *We talk by aggregates,*
And think by systems, and being used to
  face
Our evils in statistics, are inclined
To cap them with unreal remedies,
Drawn out in haste on the other side the
  slate.   *Elizabeth Barrett Browning.*

Man is a thinking being, whether he will
or no : all he can do is to turn his thoughts
the best way.   *Sir W. Temple.*

Thoughts are but dreams till their effects be tried.   *Shakespeare.*

Kindred objects kindred thoughts inspire,
As summer clouds flash forth electric fire.
                                      Rogers.

Time.

Time is the chrysalis of eternity.
                                      Richter.

I never knew the old gentleman with the
scythe and hour-glass bring anything but
grey hairs, thin cheeks, and loss of teeth.
                                      Dryden.

All that time is lost which might be
better employed.   *Rousseau.*

The inaudible and noiseless foot of time.
                                      Shakespeare.

Time is the old Justice, that examines
all offenders.   *Shakespeare.*

Who shall contend with time, unvan-
  quished time,
The conqueror of conquerors, and lord of
  desolation ?   *Kirk White.*
            Still on it creeps.
Each little moment at another's heels,
Till hours, days, years, and ages are made
  up
Of such small parts as these, and men
  look back
Worn and bewildered, wondering how it is.
Thou trav'llest like a ship in the wide
  ocean,
Which hath no bounding shore to mark its
  progress.   *Joanna Baillie.*

As every thread of gold is valuable, so is every minute of time.   *Mason.*

Dost thou love life? Then waste not time, for time is the stuff that life is made of.   *B. Franklin.*

Time, as he passes us, has a dove's wing,
Unsoil'd and swift, and of a silken sound.
     Cowper.

Title.

A fool, indeed, has great need of a title,
It teaches men to call him count and duke,
And to forget his proper name of fool.
     Crowne.

To-day.

To-day is ours: why do we fear?
To-day is ours: we have it here:
Let's banish bus'ness, banish sorrow:
To the gods belongs to-morrow.   *Cowley.*

To-morrow.

To-morrow cheats us all. Why dost thou stay,
And leave undone what should be done to-day?
Begin—the present minute's in thy power;
But still t' adjourn, and wait a fitter hour,
Is like the clown, who at some river's side
Expecting stands, in hopes the running tide
Will all ere long be past. Fool! not to know
It still has flow'd the same, and will forever flow.   *Hughes.*

Tongue.

The tongue the ambassador of the heart.
     Lyly.

Restrain thy mind, and let mildness ever attend thy tongue.   *Theognis.*

To many men well-fitting doors are not set on their tongues.   *Theognis.*

Toothache.

There was never yet philosopher
That could endure the toothache patiently.
     Shakespeare.

Treason.

Treason doth never prosper. What's the
reason?
Why, when it prospers, none dare call it
treason. *Sir John Harrington.*

Trifles.

Those who bestow too much application
on trifling things, become generally incapable of great ones. *La Rochefoucauld.*

Truth.

Truth is God's daughter.
Spanish Proverb.

He who conceals a useful truth is equally guilty with the propagator of an in-
jurious falsehood. *Augustine.*

"Truth," I cried, "though the heavens
crush me for following her; no falsehood,
though a whole celestial Lubberland were
the price of apostacy!" *Carlyle.*

Truth is a gem that is found at a great
depth; whilst on the surface of this world,
all things are weighed by the false scale
of custom. *Byron.*

There are three parts in truth: first, the
inquiry, which is the wooing of it; second-
ly, the knowledge of it, which is the presence of it; and thirdly, the belief, which
is the enjoyment of it. *Bacon.*

Truth needs no flowers of speech. *Pope.*

Twilight.

How fine to view the sun's departing ray
Fling back a lingering lovely after-day;
The moon of summer glides serenely by,
And sheds a light enchantment o'er the
sky.
These, sweetly mingling, pour upon the
sight
A pencill'd shadowing, and a dewy light—
A softened day, a half-unconscious night.
Alas! too finely pure on earth to stay,
It faintly spots the hill, and dies away.
Anon.

Tyrants.

It is worthy of observation, that the most imperious masters over their own servants, are at the same time, the most abject slaves to the servants of other masters.

Seneca.

Uncertainty.

How happy could I be with either,
Were t'other dear charmer away.

John Gay.

Unkindness.

Sharp-tooth'd unkindness. *Shakespeare.*

Unworthiness.

You are not worth the dust which the rude wind blows in your face.

Shakespeare.

Urgency.

The affair cries —haste,
And speed must answer it. *Shakespeare.*

Usurer.

A money-lender. He serves you in the present tense; he lends you in the conditional mood; keeps you in the subjunctive; and ruins you in the future!

Addison.

Utility.

Crab apples may not be the best kind of fruit; but a tree which every year bears a great crop of crab apples is better worth cultivating than a tree which bears nothing.

Valor.

The better part of valor is discretion; in the which better part I have saved my life. *Shakespeare.*

The truly valiant dare everything but doing anybody an injury.

Sir Philip Sidney.

Vanity.

She neglects her heart who studies her glass. *Lavater.*

In a vain man, the smallest spark may kindle into the greatest flame, because the materials are always prepared for it.

Hume.

Every man has just as much vanity as he wants understanding. *Pope.*

Vanity and Pride.

Pride makes us esteem ourselves; vanity makes us desire the esteem of others. It is just to say, as Dean Swift has done, that a man is too proud to be vain. *Blair.*

Variety.

Variety's the very spice of life,
That gives it all its flavor. *Cowper.*

Verbiage.

Words, words, mere words. no matter from the heart. *Shakespeare.*

Vice.

Vice repeated like the wandering wind,
Blows dust in others' eyes. *Shakespeare.*

Ah, vice! how soft are thy voluptuous ways,
While boyish blood is mantling, who can 'scape
The fascination of thy magic gaze?
A cherub-hydra round us dost thou gape,
And mould to every taste thy dear delusive shape. *Byron.*

Vice is a monster of so frightful mien,
As to be hated needs but to be seen;
Yet seen too oft, familiar with her face,
We first endure, then pity, then embrace. *Pope.*

Our pleasant vices
Are made the whip to scourge us. *Shakespeare.*

Vice stings us even in our pleasures, but virtue consoles us, even in our pains. *Colton.*

Vicissitudes.

Thus doth the ever-changing course of things
Run a perpetual circle, ever turning;
And that same day, that highest glory brings,
Brings us unto the point of back-returning. *Daniel.*

Vigilance.

The master's eye makes the horse fat.
From the Latin.

Villainy.

The evil you teach us, we will execute,
and it shall go hard but we will better the
instruction. *Shakespeare.*
He hath out-villained villainy so far,
that the rarity redeems him. *Shakespeare.*

Virtue.

The only amaranthine flow'r on earth
Is virtue; the only lasting treasure. truth.
Cowper.
A heart unspotted is not easily daunted.
Shakespeare.
And virtue is her own reward. *Prior.*

Vituperation.

The bitter clamor of two eager tongues.
Shakespeare.

Vocation.

Why, Hal, 'tis my vocation.
'Tis no sin for a man to labor in his vocation. *Shakespeare.*

Voice.

Her voice was ever soft,
Gentle. and low; an excellent thing in
woman. *Shakespeare.*

Vulgar.

To endeavor to work upon the vulgar
with fine sense, is like attempting to hew
blocks with a razor. *Pope.*

Wagers.

I've heard old cunning stagers
Say fools for arguments use wagers.
Butler.

Want.

His wit being snuft by want burnt clear.
Killigrew.

Wants.

The fewer our wants the nearer we resemble the gods. *Socrates.*

Where necessity ends, curiosity begins;
and no sooner are we supplied with every
thing that nature can demand, than we sit
down to contrive artificial appetites.

Johnson.

War.

O war! begot in pride and luxury,
The child of malice and revengeful hate;
Thou impious good, and good impiety!
Thou art the foul refiner of a state,
Unjust scourge of men's iniquity,
Sharp easer of corruptions desperate!
Is there no means but that a sin-sick land
Must be let blood with such a boist'rous
    hand?   *Daniels.*

Give me the money that has been spent
in war, and I will purchase every foot of
land upon the globe. I will clothe every
man, woman and child in an attire of
which kings and queens would be proud.
I will build a school house on every hill-
side, and in every valley over the whole
earth; I will build an academy in every
town, and endow it; a college in every
State, and fill it with able professors; I
will crown every hill with a place of worship, consecrated to the promulgation of
the gospel of peace; I will support in every
pulpit an able teacher of righteousness, so
that on every Sabbath morning the chime
on one hill should answer to the chime on
another round the earth's wide circumfer-
ence; and the voice of prayer, and the
song of praise, should ascend like an universal holocaust to heaven. *Henry Richard.*

That mad game the world so loves to
play.   *Swift.*

War, my lord,
Is of eternal use to human kind,
For ever and anon when you have pass'd
A few dull years in peace and propagation,
The world is overstock'd with fools, and
    wants
A pestilence at least if not a hero.

Jeffrey.

Warriors.

If Europe should ever be ruined, it will
be by its warriors.   *Montesquieu.*

Waste.

What maintains one vice, would bring up two children. Remember, many a little makes a mickle: and farther, beware of little expenses; a small leak will sink a great ship. *Franklin.*

Water.

Traverse the desert, and then ye can tell
What treasures exist in the cold deep well,
Sink in despair on the red parch'd earth,
And then ye may reckon what water is
     worth. *Miss Eliza Cook.*

Wealth.

It is far more easy to acquire a fortune like a knave than to expend it like a gentleman. *Colton.*

The way to wealth is as plain as the way to market. It depends chiefly on two words, industry and frugality; that is, waste neither time nor money, but make the best use of both. Without industry and frugality nothing will do, and with them everything. *Franklin.*

Wickedness.

Wickedness may prosper for awhile, but at the long run, he that sets all knaves at work will pay them. *L'Estrange.*

Wife.

What is there in the vale of life
Half so delightful as a wife;
When friendship, love, and peace combine
To stamp the marriage-bond divine?
     Cowper.

All other goods by Fortune's hand are
     given,
A wife is the peculiar gift of heaven.
     Pope.

She who ne'er answers till her husband
     cools;
Or, if she rules him, never shows she
     rules;
Charms by accepting, by submitting sways,
Yet has her humor most when she obeys.
     Pope.

Will.

In idle wishes fools supinely stay,
Be there a will,—and wisdom finds a way.
George Crabb.

Wills.

What you leave at your death, let it be
without controversy, else the lawyers will
be your heirs. *Osborne.*

Wind.

The wind has a language, I would I could
learn!
Sometimes 'tis soothing, and sometimes
'tis stern,
Sometimes it comes like a low sweet song.
And all things grow calm, as the sound
floats along,
And the forest is lull'd by the dreamy
strain,
And slumber sinks down on the wandering
main,
And its crystal arms are folded in rest,
And the tall ship sleeps on its heaving
breast. *L. E. Landon.*

Wine.

Wine is a turncoat; first a friend, and
then an enemy. *Fielding.*

Wisdom.

Common sense in an uncommon degree
is what the world calls wisdom. *Coleridge.*

It is far easier to be wise for others
than to be so for oneself.
La Rochefoucauld.

Call him wise whose actions, words and
steps are all a clear *because* to a clear *why.*
Lavater.

The wisest man is generally he who
thinks himself the least so. *Boileau.*

Wishes.

What ardently we wish we soon believe.
Young.

Wit.

Wit and judgment often are at strife,
Though meant to be each other's aid like
man and wife. *Pope.*

True wit is nature to advantage drest,
What oft was thought, but ne'er so well
    exprest,
Something whose truth, convinc'd at sight
    we find,
That gives us back the image of our mind.
                        Pope.

Woman.

'Tis beauty that doth oft make women
    proud;
'Tis virtue, that doth make them most ad-
    mired;
'Tis modesty, that makes them seem di-
    vine.   *Shakespeare.*

If the heart of a man is depress'd with
    cares,
The mist is dispelled when a woman ap-
    pears.   *Gay.*

Ould nature swears, the lovely dears
  Her noblest work she classes, O;
Her 'prentice han' she tried on man,
  An' then she made the lasses, O. *Burns.*

Woman is something between a flower
and an angel.
First, then, a woman will or won't,—de-
    pend on't;
If she will do't, she will; and there's an
    end on't,
But, if she won't, since safe and sound
    your trust is,
Fear is affront; and jealousy injustice.
                  Aaron Hill.

O woman! lovely woman! nature made
    thee
To temper man: we had been brutes with-
    out you!   *Otway.*

Women have more strength in their
looks than we have in our laws, and more
power by their tears than we have by our
arguments.   *Saville.*

O woman! in our hours of ease,
Uncertain, coy, and hard to please,
And variable as the shade
By the light quivering aspen made;
When pain and anguish wring the brow
A ministering angel thou!   *Scott.*

Woman's natural mission is to love, to love but one, to love always.   *Michelet.*

Woman knows that the better she obeys the surer she is to rule.   *Michelet.*

Woman's happiness is in obeying. She objects to men who abdicate too much.
Michelet.

Disguise our bondage as we will,
'Tis woman, woman rules us still.
Tom Moore.

What manly eloquence could produce such an effect as woman's silence.
Michelet.

He's a fool, who thinks by force, or skill,
To turn the current of a woman's will.
Tuke.

Words.

Words are men's daughters, but God's sons are things.   *Johnson.*

If you would be pungent, be brief ; for it is with words as with sunbeams—the more they are condensed the deeper they burn.
Southey.

He that uses many words for the explaining any subject, doth like the cuttle-fish, hide himself for the most part in his own ink.   *Ray.*

Words are things ; and a small drop of ink,
Failing like dew upon a thought, produces
That which makes thousands, perhaps millions, think.   *Byron.*

Apt words have power to 'suage
The tumults of a troubled mind
And are as balm to fester'd wounds.
Milton.

Working and Talking.

By work you get money, by talk you get knowledge.   *Haliburton.*

World.

O what a glory doth this world put on,
For him who with fervent heart goes forth,
Under the bright and glorious sky and looks
On duties well performed, and days well spent.   *Longfellow.*

Ay beauteous is the world, and many a joy
Floats through its wide dominion. But,
    alas,
When we would seize the winged good, it
    flies,
And step by step, along the path of life,
Allures our yearning spirits to the grave.
                   Goethe.

The world's a wood, in which all lose their
    way,
Though by a different path each goes
    astray.   *Buckingham.*

Worth.

For what is worth in anything,
But so much money as 'twill bring?
                   Butler.

Worth makes the man, and want of it the
    fellow;
The rest is all but leather or prunella.
                   Pope.

Writers.

Every great or original writer in proportion as he is great or original, must himself create the taste by which he must be
relished.   *Wordsworth.*

Writing.

           The world agrees
That he writes well who writes with ease.
                   Prior.

You write with ease to show your breeding
But easy writing's curst hard reading.
                Sheridan.

To write well is at once to think well, to
feel rightly, and to render properly! it is
to have, at the same time, mind, soul,
taste.   *Buffon.*

Years.

Winged time glides on insensibly, and
deceives us; and there is nothing more
fleeting than years.   *Ovid.*

Youth.

What is youth?—a dancing billow,
Winds behind and rocks before. *Moore.*

Crabbed age and youth
Cannot live together;
Youth is full of pleasure,
Age is full of care;
Youth like summer morn,
Age like winter weather;
Youth like summer brave,
Age like winter bare;
Youth is full of sport,
Age's breath is short;
Youth is nimble, age is lame;
Youth is hot and bold,
Age is weak and cold;
Youth is wild and age is tame.
Age, I do abhor thee;
Youth, I do adore thee;
O, my love, my love is young.
Age, I do defy thee,
O sweet shepherd, hie thee,
For methinks thou stay'st too long.
Shakespeare.

Zeal.

No wild enthusiast ever yet could rest
'Till half mankind were like himself possessed.   *Cowper.*

Famous Lines from Favorite Authors

SHAKESPEARE.

A little more than kin, and less than kind.

Seems, madam; nay, it is; I know not seems.

Frailty, thy name is woman.
Like Niobe, all tears.

O that this too, too solid flesh would melt.

Springes to catch woodcocks.

> When shall we three meet again,
> In thunder, lightning, or in rain?
> When the hurly-burly's done,
> When the battle's lost and won.

Come what come may,
Time and the hour run through the longest day.

Your face, my Thane, is as a book, where men
May read strange matters.

Letting *I dare not* wait upon *I would.*
Like the poor cat i' the adage.

I dare do all that may become a man;
Who does more, is none.

We have scotched the snake, not killed it.

Infirm of purpose!
Thou canst not say I did it; never shake
Thy gory locks at me.

Double, double, toil and trouble.

Lay on, Macduff,
And damned be he that first cries, "Hold, enough!"

One fire burns out another's burning,
One pain is lessen'd by another's anguish.

For you and I are past our dancing days.

He jests at scars that never felt a wound.

Too early seen unknown, and known too late.

Parting is such sweet sorrow.

I am the very pink of courtesy.

Adversity's sweet milk, philosophy.

Eyes, look your last;
Arms, take your last embrace.

We have seen better days.

Beware the Ides of March.

But, for mine own part, it was Greek to me.

Cowards die many times before their death,
The valiant never taste of death but once.

Though last, not least in love.

If you have tears prepare to shed them now.

This was the most unkindest cut of all.

A friend should bear his friend's infirmities,
But Brutus makes mine greater than they are.

This was the noblest Roman of them all.

I am no orator as Brutus is,
. . . I only speak right on.

One touch of nature makes the whole world kin.

So wise so young, they say, do ne'er live long.

A horse! a horse! my kingdom for a horse!

Misery acquaints a man with strange bedfellows.

He that dies pays all debts.

This is the long and short of it.

The King's English.

How use doth breed a habit in a man!

Condemn the fault, and not the actor of it.

What's mine is yours, and what is
yours is mine.

Benedick the married man.

Sets the wind in that corner?

O, what men dare do! what men may
do! what men daily do, not knowing what
they do!

Are you good men and true?

Done to death by slanderous tongues.

My cake is dough

There's small choice in rotten apples.

In maiden meditation, fancy free.

My heart
Is true as steel.
Gives to airy nothing
A local habitation and a name.

A bright particular star.

The inaudible and noiseless foot of
time.

Life is as tedious as a twice-told tale,
Vexing the dull ear of a dreaming man.

Midsummer madness.

Still you keep o' the windy side o' the
law.

I like not fair terms and a villain's
mind.

'Tis vile, unless it may be quaintly order'd,
And better, in my mind, not undertook.

Who chooseth me shall gain what many
men desire.

Who chooseth me shall get as much as
he deserves.

Who chooseth me must give or hazard
all he hath.

I will assume desert.

O, these deliberate fools! when they do
choose,
They have the wisdom by their wit to
lose.

What, wouldst thou have a serpent
sting thee twice?

A Daniel come to judgment!
O wise and upright judge.
How much more elder art thou than thy
looks!

Is it so nominated in the bond?

I cannot find it; 'tis not in the bond.

A Daniel, still say I, a second Daniel!
I thank thee, Jew, for teaching me that
word.

He is well paid that is well satisfied.
Sir, you are very welcome to our house;
It must appear in other ways than words,
·Therefore I scant this breathing courtesy.

Motley's the only wear.

I had rather have a fool to make me
merry, than experience to make me sad.

The Retort Courteous.—The Lie Cir-
cumstantial.—The Lie Direct.

Good wine needs no bush.

Your *If* is the only peacemaker; much
virtue in *If*.

The ripest fruit first falls.

He will give the devil his due.

I know a trick worth two of that.

It would be argument for a week,
laughter for a month, and a good jest forever.

Brain him with a lady's fan.

A good mouth-filling oath.

Shall I not take mine ease in mine inn?

I could have better spared a better man.

He hath eaten me out of house and
home.

Uneasy lies the head that wears a
crown.

Thy wish was father, Harry, to that
thought

How sharper than a serpent's tooth it is
To have a thankless child!

Striving to better, oft we mar what's
well.

I am a man
More sinned against than sinning.

O, that way madness lies; let me shun
that.

The little dogs and all,
Tray, Blanche, and Sweetheart, see, they
 bark at me.

Ay, every inch a king.
But I will wear my heart upon my sleeve
For daws to peck at.

Put money in thy purse.

Framed to make women false.

For I am nothing, if not critical.

Iago.—What, are you hurt, lieutenant?

Cas.—Ay, past all surgery.

O thou invisible spirit of wine, if thou
hast no name to be known by, let us call
thee devil!

O that men should put an enemy in
their mouths to steal away their brains!

Trifles, light as air,
Are to the jealous confirmations strong
As proofs of holy writ.

Speak of me as I am; nothing extenuate,
Nor set down aught in malice; then must
 you speak
Of one that lov'd, not wisely, but too well.

My salad days,
When I was green in judgment.

It beggared all description.

Age cannot wither her, nor custom stale
Her infinite variety.

Let's do it after the high Roman fashion.

As it fell upon a day
In the merry month of May.

We are such stuff
As dreams are made on, and our little life
Is rounded with a sleep.

JONATHAN SWIFT.

Bread is the staff of life.

No wise man ever wished to be younger.

I shall be like that tree; I shall die at
the top.

EDWARD YOUNG.

At thirty man suspects himself a fool;
Knows it at forty and reforms his plan.
   Be wise with speed;
 A fool at forty is a fool indeed.

How blessings brighten as they take their flight.

Wishing, of all employments, is the worst.

And all may do what has by man been done.

   Beautiful as sweet!
And young as beautiful! and soft as young
And gay as soft! and innocent as gay!

'Tis impious in a good man to be sad.

JOHN DRYDEN.

None but the brave deserve the fair.

And like another Helen, fired another Troy.

Who think too little, and who talk too much.

Everything by starts, and nothing long.

The young men's vision, and the old men's dream.

She hugged the offender and forgave the offense.

Sex to the last.

For Art may err, but Nature cannot miss.

Errors, like straws, upon the surface flow;
He who would search for pearls must dive below.

All delays are dangerous in war.

ALEXANDER POPE.

Thou wert my guide, philosopher, and friend.

'Tis education forms the common mind:
Just as the twig is bent the tree's inclined.

Odious! in woolen! 'twould a saint provoke!

Who shall decide when doctors disagree,
And soundest causists doubt, like you and me?

Heaven from all creatures hides the book of fate.

Shoot folly as it flies.

Lo, the poor Indian! whose untutored mind
Sees God in clouds, or hears Him in the wind.

Honor and shame from no condition rise;
Act well your part, there all the honor lies.

Curst be the verse, how well soe'er it flow,
That tends to make one worthy man my foe.

There St. John mingles with my friendly bowl,
The feast of reason, and the flow of soul.

Welcome the coming, speed the departing guest.

The last and greatest art, the art to blot.

I am his Highness' dog at Kew,
Pray tell me, sir, whose dog are you?

Thou great First Cause, least understood.

Whatever is, is right.

JOHN MILTON.

Tears, such as angels weep, burst forth.

Which, if not victory, is yet revenge.

The bright consummate flower.

Deep-versed in books and shallow in himself.

When more is meant than meets the ear.

The oracles are dumb.

That old man eloquent.

License they mean when they cry liberty.

JOSEPH ADDISON.

My voice is still for war,
Gods! can a Roman senate long debate
Which of the two to choose, slavery or
    death?

A day, an hour, of virtuous liberty
Is worth a whole eternity in bondage.

The woman who deliberates is lost.

The spacious firmament on high,
With all the blue ethereal sky—
    .   .   .   .

Forever singing, as they shine,
The hand that made us is divine.

EDMUND BURKE.

There is, however, a limit at which forbearance ceases to be a virtue.

But the age of chivalry is gone.   That
of sophisters, economists, and calculators
has succeeded.

Early and provident fear is the mother
of safety.

WILLIAM COWPER.

England, with all thy faults, I love thee
    still,
My country!

She that asks
Her dear five hundred friends.

The beggarly last doit.

A fool must now and then be right by
chance.

A hat not much the worse for wear.

And Satan trembles when he sees
The weakest saint upon his knees.

Beware of desperate steps.   The darkest
    day,
Live till to-morrow, will have passed
    away.

OLIVER GOLDSMITH.

And learn the luxury of doing good.

These little things are great to little man.

But winter lingering, chills the lap of May.

He cast off his friends, as a huntsman his
    pack,
For he knew, when he choosed, he could
    whistle them back.

SAMUEL TAYLOR COLERIDGE.

As idle as a painted ship
Upon a painted ocean.

Water, water, everywhere,
Nor any drop to drink.

A sadder and a wiser man
He rose the morrow morn.

He prayeth best, who loveth best
All things, both great and small.

A sight to dream of, not to tell.

Alas! they had been friends in youth;
But whispering tongues can poison truth;
And constancy lives in realms above;
    And life is thorny, and youth is vain,
And to be wroth with one we love,
    Doth work like madness in the brain.

Motionless torrents! silent cataracts!
Ye living flowers that skirt the eternal
    frost.

Our myriad-minded Shakespeare.

A dwarf sees father than the giant
when he has the giant's shoulder to mount
on.

THOMAS CAMPBELL.

'Tis distance lends enchantment to the
    view,
And robes the mountain in its azure hue.

The combat deepens. On, ye brave,
Who rush to glory or the grave!

To bear is to conquer our fate.

223

LORD BYRON.

'Tis pleasant, sure, to see one's name in
    print;
A book's a book, although there's nothing
    in't.

With just enough of learning to mis-
quote.

    Maid of Athens, ere we part,
    Give, oh! give me back my heart.

Had sighed to many, though he loved
but one.

The dome of Thought, the palace of the
Soul.

Hereditary bondsmen! know ye not,
Who would be free, themselves must
    strike the blow.

Music arose with its voluptuous swell—
Soft eyes looked love to eyes which spake
    again,
    And all went merry as a marriage bell.

On with the dance! let joy be uncon-
fined.

And there was mounting in hot haste.

I stood in Venice, on the Bridge of Sighs;
A palace and a prison on each hand.

                  Man!
Thou pendulum betwixt a smile and tear.

"While stands the Coliseum Rome shall
    stand;
When falls the Coliseum, Rome shall fall;
And when Rome falls—the world."

I die—but first I have possess'd,
And come what may, I have been blest.

He makes a solitude, and calls it—
peace.

Hark! to the hurried question of despair,
"Where is my child?"—an Echo answers
    —"Where?"

The power of Thought—the magic of
the mind.

And both were young, and one was
beautiful.

A change came o'er the spirit of my
dream.

My boat is on the shore
And my bark is on the sea.

The precious porcelain of common clay.

Society is now one polished horde.
Formed of two mighty tribes, the Bores,
and Bored.

I awoke one morning and found myself
famous.

The best of Prophets of the future is
the Past.

And what is writ, is writ—
Would it were worthier?

JOHN KEATS.

Philosophy will clip an angel's wings.

Thou foster-child of Silence and slow
Time.

TALLEYRAND.

Prudence in women should be an instinct, not a virtue.

What I have been taught I have forgotten; what I know I have guessed.

The love of glory can only create a
hero: the contempt of it creates a great
man.

If you wish to appear agreeable in society, you must consent to be taught many
things which you know already.

There are two things to which we never
grow accustomed—the ravages of time
and the injustice of our fellow-men.

He who cannot feel friendship is alike
incapable of love. Let a woman beware
of the man who owns that he loves no
one but herself.

It is sometimes quite enough for a man
to feign ignorance of that which he
knows, to gain the reputation of knowing
that of which he is ignorant.

Human life is like a game of chess—
each piece holds its place upon the chessboard—king, queen, bishop, and pawn.
Death comes, the game is up, and all are
thrown, without distinction, pell-mell in
the same bag.

CHARLES DICKENS.

In a Pickwickian sense.

When found, make a note of.

My life is one demd horrid grind.

Barkis is willin'.

Lor! let's be comfortable.

In came Mrs. Fezziweg, one vast substantial smile.

Oh! a dainty plant is the ivy green,
  That creepeth o'er ruins old!
Of right choice food are his meals, ween,
  In his cell so lone and cold.
Creeping where no life is seen,
A rare old plant is the ivy green.

Miscellaneous Quotations.

Build thee more stately mansions, O **my**
    soul,
       As the swift seasons roll!
       Leave thy low vaulted past!
Let each new temple, nobler than the last,
Shut thee from heaven with a dome more
    vast,
       Till thou at last art free,
Leaving thine outgrown shell by life's un-
    resting sea.   *O. W. Holmes.*

    For myself alone I doubt;
    All is well, I know, without;
    I alone the beauty mar,
    I alone the music jar.
    Yet with hands by evil stained,
    And an ear by discord pained,
    I am groping for the keys
    Of the heavenly harmonies.
                J. G. Whittier.

      Into the sunshine,
        Full of the light,
      Leaping and flashing
        From morn till night!

   .   .   .   .   .

      Glorious fountain!
        Let my heart be
    Fresh, changeful, constant,
        Upward, like thee!
                J. R. Lowell.

    I knew a very wise man that believed
that if a man were permitted to make all
the ballads he need not care who should
make the laws of a nation.
                Andrew Fletcher.

Then gently scan your brother man,
    Still gentler, sister woman;
Though they may gang a kennin wrang,
    To step aside is human.

   .   .   .   .   .

What's done we partly may compute,
    But know not what's resisted. **Burns.**

> Alas for the rarity
> Of Christian charity
> Under the sun!   *Thomas Hood.*

> Like the dew on the mountain,
>   Like the foam on the river,
> Like the bubble on the fountain,
>   Thou art gone, and forever!   *Scott.*

Philosophy is the romance of the aged,
and Religion the only future history for
us all.   *Balbi, Life and Times of Dante.*

Boston State House is the hub of the
Solar System. You couldn't pry that out
of a Boston man if you had the tire of all
creation straightened out for a crowbar.
                    O. W. Holmes, Autocrat.

Say—the world is a nettle; disturb it, it
    stings :
Grasp it firmly, it stings not. On one of
    two things,
If you would not be stung, it behooves
    you to settle :
Avoid it, or crush it.   *Owen Meredith.*

> Tender-handed grasp a nettel
>   And it stings you for your pains ;
> Grasp it like a man of mettle
>   And it soft as silk remains.
>   *Aaron Hill.*

Every man has in himself a continent of
undiscovered character. Happy he who
acts the Columbus to his own soul!
                    Stephen.

Conquering, not as anger is cowed by
fiercer anger, or hate by bitterer hate, but
as anger is subdued by patience and hatred is conquered by love. And the con-
quests of patience and love are slow.
        Author of Schonberg-Cotta Family.

O noble conscience, upright and refined,
How slight a fault inflicts a bitter sting.
        Dante, Purgatorio III, Wright, Tr.

Nature fits all her children with something
    to do,
He who would write and can't write, can
    surely review.   *J. R. Lowell*

Meanwhile the guilty soul cannot keep its own secret. It is false to itself; or, rather, it feels an irresistible impulse of conscience to be true to itself. . . . It must be confessed—it *will* be confessed—there is no refuge from confession but suicide, and suicide is confession.

Daniel Webster, in the Knapp Trial.

How sink the brave who sink to rest,
By all their country's wishes blest!

. . . . .

By fairy hands their knell is rung;
By forms unseen their dirge is sung.
There Honor comes, a pilgrim gray,
To bless the turf that wraps their clay;
And Freedom shall awhile repair,
To dwell a weeping hermit there.

Collins.

Was it something said,
  Something done,
Vexed him? was it touch of hand,
  Turn of head?
Strange! that very way
  Love began.
I as little understand
  Love's decay.   *Robert Browning.*

The mossy marbles rest
On the lips that he has prest
  In their bloom:
And the names he loved to hear
Have been carved for many a year
  On the tomb.   *O. W. Holmes.*

We may live without poetry, music, and
  art;
We may live without conscience, and live
  without heart;
We may live without friends; we may live
  without books;
But civilized man cannot live without
  cooks.
He may live without books—what is knowledge but grieving?
He may live without hope—what is hope
  but deceiving?
He may live without love—what is passion
  but pining?
But where is the man that can live without dining.   *Owen Meredith.*

Not a drum was heard, not a funeral note,
As his corpse to the rampart we hurried.

.   .   .   .   .

But he lay like a warrior taking his rest,
With his martial cloak around him.

.   .   .   .   .

We carved not a line, and we raised not a
stone,
But we left him alone in his glory.
*Charles Wolfe, The Burial of Sir John
Moore.*

The consciousness of clean linen is in
and of itself a source of moral strength
only second to that of a clean conscience.
A well-ironed collar, or a fresh glove, has
carried many a man through the emer-
gency in which a wrinkle or a rip would
have defeated him.   *E. S. Phelps.*

Grant me, O sweet and loving Jesus, to
rest in Thee, above all other creatures,
above all health and beauty, above all glory
and honour, above all power and dignity,
above all knowledge and subtlety, above all
riches and arts, above all joy and glad-
ness, above all fame and praise, above all
sweetness and comfort, above all hope
and promise, above all desert and desire,
above all gifts and benefits that Thou
canst give and impart unto us, above all
mirth and joy that the mind of man can
receive and feel; finally, above angels and
archangels, and above all the heavenly
host, above all things visible and invisible,
and above all that Thou art not, O my
God.   *Thomas à Kempis.*

Within that awful volume lies
The mystery of mysteries!

.   .   .   .   .

And better had they ne'er been born,
Who read to doubt, or read to scorn.
          Scott.

The paths of glory lead but to the grave.
          Gray's Elegy.

A dull mind, once arriving at an inference that flatters a desire, is rarely able
to retain the impression that the notion
from which the inference started was
purely problematic.   *George Eliot.*

Sometimes, I think, the things we see
Are shadows of the things to be:
  That what we plan we build;
That every hope that hath been crossed,
And every dream we thought was lost,
  In Heaven shall be fulfilled.
Phoebe Cary.

Life! we have been long together,
Through pleasant and through cloudy
     weather;
'Tis hard to part when friends are dear;
Perhaps 'twill cost a sigh, a tear ·
Then steal away, give little warning,
Choose thine own time:
Say not "Good night," but in some bright-
    er clime
Bid me "Good mornin." *Mrs. Barbauld.*

The love of Ophelia, which she never
once confesses, is like a secret which we
have stolen from her, and which ought to
die upon our hearts as upon her own.
Mrs. Jamison.

When love and skill work together, expect a masterpiece.   *Charles Reade.*

Love feels no burden, thinks nothing of
trouble, attempts what is above its
strength, pleads no excuse of impossibility;
for it thinks all things lawful for itself,
and all things possible.

It is therefore able to undertake all
things, and it completes many things, and
brings them to a conclusion, where he who
does not love, faints and lies down.
Thomas à Kempis.

Shall I, wasting in despair,
Die because a woman's fair?
Or make pale my cheeks with care,
'Cause another's rosy are?

Be she fairer than the day,
Or the flowery meads in May,
If she be not so to me,
What care I how fair she be?
George Wither.

I could not love thee, dear, so much,
Loved I not honor more.
Richard Lovelace.

Where true love has found a home,
every new year forms one more ring
around the hearts of those who love each
other, so that in the end they cannot live
apart.   *Julius Stinde.*

Fain would I climb, yet fear I to fall.
                         Sir Walter Raleigh.

If thy heart fails thee, climb not at all.
                         Queen Elizabeth's reply.

No mistress of the hidden skill,
   No wizard gaunt and grim,
Went up by night on heath or hill
   To read the stars for him;
But the merriest maid in all the land
   Of vine-encircled France
Bestowed upon his brow and hand
   Her philosophic glance:
"I bind thee with a spell," said she,
   "I sign thee with a sign;
No woman's love shall light on thee,
   No woman's heart be thine!"
      Mrs. Hemans, The Child's Destiny.

I remember, I remember,
   How my childhood fleeted by
The mirth of its December,
   And the warmth of its July.
                    W. M. Praed.

I love it, I love it, and who shall dare
To chide me for loving that old arm-
      chair?   *Eliza Cook.*

Oft in the stilly night,
Ere slumber's chain has bound me,
Fond memory brings the light
   Of others days around me!
      The smiles, the tears
      Of boyhood's years,
The words of love then spoken;
      The eyes that shone,
      Now dimmed and gone,
The cheerful hearts now broken!

      .   .   .   .   .   .
   I feel like one
   Who treads alone
Some banquet-hall deserted,
   Whose lights are fled,
   Whose garlands dead,
And all but he departed!
                    Thomas Moore.

The old oaken bucket, the iron-bound
   bucket,
The moss-covered bucket, which hung in
   the well.   *Samuel Woodworth.*

Near the lake where drooped the willow,
    Long time ago!   *George P. Morris.*
     Woodman, spare that tree!
      Touch not a single bough!
    In youth it sheltered me,
     And I'll protect it now.
         George P. Morris.

    When the sun sinks to rest,
    And the star of the west
Sheds its soft silver light o'er the sea,
    What sweet thoughts arise,
    As the dim twilight dies—
For then I am thinking of thee!
    O! then crowding fast
    Come the joys of the past,
Through the dimness of days long gone
   by,
    Like the stars peeping out,
    Through the darkness about,
From the soft silent depth of the sky.

    And thus, as the night
    Grows more lovely and bright
With the clustering of planet and star,
    So this darkness of mine
    Wins a radiance divine
From the light that still lingers afar.
    Then welcome the night,
    With its soft holy light!
In its silence my heart is more free
    The rude world to forget,
    Where no pleasure I've met
Since the hour that I parted from thee.
         Samuel Lover.

Through days of sorrow and of mirth,
Through days of death and days of birth,
Through every swift vicissitude
Of changeful time, unchanged it has
   stood.
And as if, like God, it all things saw,
It calmly repeats those words of awe—
    "Forever—never!
    Never—forever!"
     Longfellow, The Old Clock.

Stone walls do not a prison make,
　Nor iron bars a cage;
Minds innocent and quiet take
　That for an hermitage.
Richard Lovelace.

Could we forbear dispute and practice
　love,
We should agree as angels do above.
Waller.

I hold every man a debtor to his profession; from the which as men of course
do seek to receive countenance and profit,
so ought they of duty to endeavor themselves by way of amends to be a help
and ornament thereunto. *Bacon.*

Music hath charms to soothe the savage
　breast,
To soften rocks, or bend a knotted oak,
By magic numbers and persuasive sound.
Congreve.

When Music, heavenly maid. was young,
While yet in early Greece she sung.

　　　·　　·　　·　　·　　·

Filled with fury, rapt, inspired,

　　·　　·　　·　　·　　·

'Twas sad by fits, by starts 'twas wild.

　·　　·　　·　　·　　·

In notes by distance made more sweet,
In hollow murmurs died away.

　　·　　·　　·　　·

O Music! sphere-descended maid,
Friend of pleasure, wisdom's aid.
William Collins, Ode to the Passions.

Come forth unto the light of things,
　Let Nature be your teacher.

　·　　·　　·　　·　　·　　·

One impulse from a vernal wood
May teach you more of man,
Of moral evil and of good,
　Than all the sages can. *Wordsworth.*

The melancholy days are come, the sad-
　dest of the year,
Of wailing winds, and naked woods, and
　meadows brown and sere.
Heaped in the hollows of the grove the
　withered leaves lie dead.
They rustle to the eddying gust, and to
　the rabbit's tread. *W. C. Bryant.*

Nature, before it has been touched by man, is almost always beautiful, strong, and cheerful in man's eyes; but nature, when he has once given it his culture and then forsakes it, has usually an air of sorrow and helplessness. He has made it live the more by laying his hand upon it, and touching it with his life. It has come to relish of his humanity, and it is so flavored with his thoughts, and ordered and permeated by his spirit, that if the stimulus of his presence is withdrawn it cannot for a long while do without him, and live for itself as fully and as well as it did before.　　*Jean Ingelow.*

The sea! the sea! the open sea!
The blue, the fresh, the ever free!
Without a mark, without a bound,
It runneth the earth's wide region round.

　.　　.　　.　　.　　.　　.

I never was on the dull, tame shore,
But I loved the great sea more and more,
And backward flew to her billowy breast,
Like a bird that seeketh its mother's
　　nest.　　　*Bryan W. Procter.*

Like a spear of flame the cardinal flower
Burned out along the meadow.　　*Eddy.*

A strong nor'wester's blowing, Bill;
　Hark! don't ye hear it roar now!
Lord help 'em, how I pities them
　Unhappy folks on shore now!
William Pitt, The Sailor's Consolation.

Dearest, has Heaven aught to give thee
　more?
　I thought the while I watched her
　changing face,
　Heard her fine tones and marked her
　gestures' grace—
Yea, one more gift is left all gifts be-
　fore.

We go our separate ways on earth, and
　pain,
　God's shaping chisel, waits us as the
　rest,
　With nobler charm thy beauty to invest,
And make thee lovelier ere we meet again.
　　　　Celia Thaxter

Not perfect, nay, but full of tender wants
No angel, but a dearer being, all dipt
In angel instincts, breathing Paradise.
Tennyson.

Sink or swim, live or die, survive or
perish, I give my heart and my hand to
this vote. *Webster.*

The Guard dies, but never surrenders.
Rougemont.

There is one certain means by which I
can be sure never to see my country's
ruin—*I will die in the last ditch.*
William of Orange.

Cæsar had his Brutus—Charles the
First, his Cromwell—and George the
Third ("Treason!" cried the Speaker)—
may profit by their example. If *this* be
treason, make the most of it.
Patrick Henry, Speech, 1765.

Praise the Power that hath made and
    preserved us a nation!
Then conquer we must, when our cause
    it is just,
And this be our motto: "In God is our
    trust;"
And the star-spangled banner, O long may
    it wave
O'er the land of the free, and the home
    of the brave. *Francis Scott Key.*

Forever floats that standard sheet!
    Where breathes the foe but falls before
    us,
With Freedom's soil beneath our feet,
    And Freedom's banner streaming o'er
    us. *Joseph Rodman Drake.*

Give me liberty or give me death!
Patrick Henry.

A song for our banner? The watchword
    recall
Which gave the Republic her station:
"United we stand—divided we fall!"
    It made and preserves us a nation!
The union of lakes—the union of lands—
    The union of States none can sever—
The union of hearts, the union of hands—
    And the flag of our Union forever!
George P. Morris.

O rally 'round the flag, boys, rally once
  again,
Shouting the battle-cry of Freedom.
> *George F. Root.*

We join ourselves to no party that does
not carry the flag and keep step to the
music of the Union. *Rufus Choate.*

When can their glory fade?
Oh! the wild charge they made!
  All the world wondered.
Honour the charge they made!
Honour the Light Brigade,
  Noble six hundred! *Tennyson.*

And he gave it as his opinion, that
whoever could make two ears of corn, or
two blades of grass, to grow upon a spot
of ground where only one grew before,
would deserve better of mankind, and
do more essential service to his country,
than the whole race of politicians put together. *Swift, Gulliver's Travels.*

I never could believe that Providence
had sent a few men into the world ready
booted and spurred to ride, and millions
ready saddled and bridled to be ridden.
> *Richard Rumbold, on the scaffold.*

Millions for defense, but not one cent
for tribute. *C. C. Pinckney.*

To the memory of the man, first in
war, first in peace, and first in the hearts
of his country. *General Henry Lee.*

But whether on the scaffold high,
  Or in the battle's van,
The fittest place where man can die
  Is where he dies for man.
> *Michael J. Barry.*

Let the soldier be abroad if he will, he
can do nothing in this age. There is another personage, a personage less impos-
ing in the eyes of some, perhaps insignifi-
cant. The schoolmaster is abroad, and I
trust to him, armed with his primer,
against the soldier in full military array.
> *Lord Brougham.*

O for a seat in some poetic nook,
Just hid with trees, and sparkling with a
  brook. *Leigh Hunt.*

In winter, when the dismal rain
  Came slanting down in lines,
And Wind, that grand old harper, smote
  His thunder-harp of pines.
Alexander Smith.

There were two or three pretty faces
among the female singers, to which the
keen air of a frosty morning had given a
bright rosy tint ; but the gentlemen choristers
had evidently been chosen, like old Cre-
mona fiddles, more for tone than looks ;
and as several had to sing from the same
book, there were clusterings of odd phys-
iognomies, not unlike those groups of
cherubs we sometimes see on country
tombstones.   *Irving.*

Seemed washing his hands with invisible
  soap
  In imperceptible water.   *Hood.*

Reason is the life of the law ; nay, the
common law itself is nothing else but
reason. . . . The law which is the
perfection of reason.   *Coke.*

           Remorse—she ne'er forsakes us—
A bloodhound staunch—she tracks our
  rapid step
Through the wild labyrinth of youthful
  frenzy,
Unheard, perchance, until old age hath
  tamed us ;
Then in our lair, when Time hath chilled
  our joints,
And maimed our hope of combat, or of
  flight,
We hear her deep-mouthed bay, announc-
  ing all
Of wrath, and woe, and punishment that
  bides us.   *Old Play*

Do what lieth in thy power, and God
will assist in thy good will.
Thomas à Kempis.

Weep no more, lady, weep no more,
  Thy sorrow is in vain ;
For violets plucked, the sweetest showers
  Will ne'er make grow again.
John Fletcher.

God will not give any soldier ammunition who is not willing to go into battle.
Anon.

What does little baby say,
In her bed at peep of day?
Baby says, like little birdie,
Let me rise and fly away.

Baby, sleep a little longer,
Till the little limbs are stronger.
If she sleeps a little longer
Baby, too, shall fly away.
Tennyson, Cradle Song in Sea Dreams.

Sweet and low, sweet and low,
  Wind of the western sea,
Low. low, breathe and blow,
  Wind of the western sea!
Over the rolling waters go,
Come from the dying moon and blow,
  Blow him again to me:
While my little one, while my pretty one,
  sleeps.

Sleep and rest, sleep and rest,
  Father will come to thee soon;
Rest, rest, on mother's breast,
  Father will come to thee soon;
Father will come to his babe in the nest,
Silver sails all out of the west,
  Under the silver moon:
Sleep, my little one, sleep, my pretty one,
  sleep.   *Tennyson, The Princess.*

Were I to adopt a pet idea as so many people do, and fondle it in my embraces to the exclusion of all others, it would be, that the great want which mankind labors under at this present period is sleep. The world should recline its vast head on the first convenient pillow and take an age-long nap. It has gone distracted through a morbid activity, and, while preternaturally wide awake, is nevertheless tormented by visions that seem real to it now, but would assume their true aspect and character were all things once set right by an interval of sound repose.

Hawthorne, Mosses from an Old Manse.

Oh! would I were dead now
Or up in my bed now,
To cover my head now,
And have a good cry!
Thomas Hood.

When death, the great Reconciler, has come, it is never our tenderness that we repent of, but our severity. *George Eliot.*

My best thoughts always come a little too late. *Hawthorne.*

Thought is deeper than all speech;
Feeling deeper than all thought;
Souls to souls can never teach
What unto themselves was taught.
Christopher P. Cranch.

Too late I stayed—forgive the crime—
Unheeded flew the hours;
How noiseless falls the foot of time,
That only treads on flowers.
Wm. Robt. Spencer.

Gather ye rosebuds while ye may,
Old Time is still a-flying,
And this same flower that smiles to-day,
To-morrow may be dying.
Robert Herrick.

O! a wonderful stream is the river Time,
As it runs through the realm of tears!
With a faultless rhythm, and a musical rhyme,
And a broader sweep and a surge sublime,
As it blends in the ocean of years!
B. F. Taylor.

By Woden, God of Saxons,
From whom comes Wensday, that is, Wednesday,
Truth is a thing that I will ever keep
Unto thylke day in which I creep into
My sepulcre. *Cartwright's Ordinary.*

O God, who art the truth, make me one with Thee in everlasting love.
Thomas à Kempis.